The Early Childhood Inclusive Education Checklist:

A Self-Assessment of Best Practices

by
Jacqueline S. Thousand, Ph.D.
& Richard A. Villa, Ed.D.

National Professional Resources, Inc.
Naples, FL

The Early Childhood Inclusive Education Checklist: A Self-Assessment of Best Practices

Library of Congress Control Number: 2019947558

Printed in the United States of America on acid-free paper

ISBN 9781949961102

National Professional Resources, Inc.
Naples, FL

For information:
National Professional Resources, Inc.
1455 Rail Head Blvd., Suite 6
Naples, FL 34110
www.NPRinc.com
Phone: (800) 453-7461

Cover Design: Jaclyn Falk
Editorial Production: Andrea Cerone
Executive Editor: Lisa Hanson

Contents

About the Authors

Jacqueline S. Thousand is professor emerita at California State University San Marcos and vice president of Bayridge Consortium. She has developed and coordinated Education Specialist credential and Master of Arts programs and spearheaded the establishment of co-teaching as the clinical practice paradigm for all teacher preparation programs in the School of Education. She is a noted inclusive education advocate who has co-authored 28 books and numerous research articles and chapters on issues related to culturally proficient inclusive schooling, co-teaching, organizational change strategies, differentiated instruction and universal design, cooperative learning, collaborative teaming and creative problem-solving processes, student self-determination, and discipline with dignity. She is actively involved in international teacher education and inclusive education endeavors and serves on the editorial and advisory boards of several national and international journals and professional organizations.

Dr. Jacqueline S. Thousand
Professor, California State University San Marcos
333 South Twin Oaks Valley Road
San Marcos, CA 92096
760-533-1744 ~ jthousan@csusm.edu

Richard A. Villa, president of Bayridge Consortium Inc., is an internationally known expert on the development of support systems for educating all students in general education. Dr. Villa has served as a middle and high school social studies, science, special education, and Title 1 teacher; a special education coordinator; a director of pupil personnel services; and a director of curriculum and instruction. He has co-authored 27 books and over 100 chapters and journal articles on topics from co-teaching and differentiated instruction to inclusion and leadership in school reform and restructuring. Dr. Villa is a highly sought-after district, state, national and international professional development presenter, consultant, and coach. He is known for his knowledgeable, enthusiastic, audience-engaging, and humorous presentation style. Additional information about Dr. Villa can be found at his website, www.ravillabayridge.com.

Dr. Richard A. Villa
President, Bayridge Consortium, Inc.
113 West G Street, Suite 444
San Diego, CA 92101
619-795-3602 ~ ravillabayridge@cs.com
www.ravillabayridge.com

Introduction

The Early Childhood Inclusive Education Checklist: A Self-Assessment of Best Practices is designed to communicate the what, why, and how of early childhood inclusive education, and provide readers with best practice indicators that will assist them in assessing their current level of implementation of best practices and planning for continuous improvement. It is our belief that if home, school, and community partners share the information in this book and conduct self-assessments related to the best practices described herein, it will create common conceptual frameworks, knowledge, and skills among the stakeholders and result in increased opportunities for young children to flourish in inclusive environments. In this introduction, we: a) briefly define and provide rationale for early childhood inclusive education; b) identify 13 early childhood inclusive education best practices; c) offer a pyramid model conceptual framework to explain how best practices work together to ensure access, participation, supports, and success for young children in early childhood inclusive educational environments; and d) explain how to use the indicators included with each of the 13 best practices to assess current level of implementation of the indicators and plan for improvement.

What is Early Childhood Inclusive Education?

Inclusive education for preschool and school-aged children can be defined as both the vision and practice of welcoming, valuing, empowering, and supporting the diverse academic, social-emotional, language, and communication learning of all students in shared environments and experiences for the purpose of attaining the desired goals of education (Villa & Thousand, 2016). The joint position statement on inclusion (2009) by the Council for Exceptional Children's Division for Early Childhood (DEC) and the National Association for the Education of Young Children (NAEYC) further clarifies inclusive education as it applies in early childhood, identifying access, participation, and supports as the three defining features of high quality inclusive early childhood programs and services.

Why Create Early Childhood Inclusive Environments?

Research findings overwhelmingly favor inclusive versus disability-only educational experiences for children eligible for early childhood special education services and supports (Strain & Smith, 2016). Inclusive settings provide higher quality learning experiences, resulting in superior student learning. Children's communication and cognitive skill development are greater in inclusive settings, with the greatest growth in the social domain. Further, positive outcomes cut across the range of disability categories, varying intensity of support needs, and types of inclusive early childhood education and care settings.

What Early Childhood Inclusive Education Best Practices Are Assessed in *The Early Childhood Inclusive Education Checklist?*

Chapters 1 though 13 describe and provide best practice indicators for the following 13 early childhood inclusive education best practices, which represent a checklist of essential components of quality early childhood inclusive education:

1. Understanding What Early Childhood Inclusion Is
2. Home-School-Community Collaboration
3. Redefined Roles and Responsibilities of Early Childhood Educators and Community Care Providers; Special Educators, Related Services Personnel, and Other Support and Health Specialists; and Paraeducators
4. Collaborative Teaming
5. Co-teaching
6. Structuring Intentional, Sufficient, and Supported Natural Peer Interactions
7. Student-Centered, Strength-Based Assessment and Differentiated Instruction
8. Multi-Tiered System of Supports (MTSS) for Differentiated, Embedded, Specially Designed, and Targeted Instruction, and Academic, Behavioral, and Social-Emotional Learning
9. Decision-Making Processes for Determining Where, When, and How to Address IEP Goals for Students with Intensive and Pervasive Support Needs
10. Professional Learning and Coaching
11. Administrative Practices Supportive of Early Childhood Inclusive Education
12. Transition Planning from Part C (Birth to Three) to Part B (Three to Five) Services, and from Part B (Three to Five) to School-Aged Services
13. Continuous Planning for Sustainability

A Pyramid Model for Designing Early Childhood Inclusive Educational Environments and Experiences

Figure 1 (page 13) presents an Early Childhood Inclusive Education Pyramid Model that illustrates how the 13 best practices featured in this book interrelate and build upon one another to achieve the overarching goals of access, participation, supports, and success for all young children. The five-tiered pyramid framework has as its foundation/ first tier strong administrative leadership and support. Three best practices—Best Practices 10, 11 and 13—examine key dimensions of administrative leadership and support. Best Practice 11, Administrative Practices Supportive of Inclusive Early Childhood Education, describes actions administrators can take to orchestrate change and progress in education by attending to five change variables: vision, skills, incentives, resources, and action planning. Best Practice 10, Professional Learning and Coaching, focuses upon the skills change variable, describing the knowledge, skills, coaching, and mentorship early childhood instructional personnel and community partners need to effectively plan for and instruct young children with and without IEPs. Best Practice 13, Continuous Planning for Sustainability, elaborates upon the action planning change variable, offering a planning tool to ensure attention to all five change variables.

The second tier of the pyramid, Collaborative Planning & Creative Problem Solving, acknowledges collaboration and creative problem solving as essential processes for actualizing change. Although collaboration and creative problem solving are needed to implement all of the 13 best practices described in this book, they are particularly critical to four practices included at this second tier. Best Practice 2, Home-School-Community Collaboration, acknowledges that young children receive care and education in multiple home, community, and school-based settings, necessitating communication to coordinate supports and services. Best Practice 3, Redefined Roles and Responsibilities, describes how the roles of everyone providing instruction, care, and support to young children in inclusive environments change to be essentially collaborative. Best Practice 4, Collaborative Teaming, offers strategies for optimizing collaborative planning among adults supporting young children. Best Practice 12, Transition Planning, emphasizes the importance of careful and deliberate collaboration and planning during times of transition in order to achieve continuity for children and families and across systems.

The third tier of the pyramid model, Organizational Structures, is shared by three organizational structures and processes for marshaling and deploying human resources to increase the likelihood of curricular and instructional differentiation for young children with diverse learning profiles. Best Practice 8, Multi-Tiered System of Supports (MTSS), describes an overarching structure for organizing support for the academic and social-emotional-behavioral health and growth of children by automatically differentiating instruction based upon the natural learning differences among children. Essential to the implementation of MTSS is the bringing together of human resources through the co-teaching arrangements and practices described in Best Practice 5, Co-Teaching. Also included in Tier 3 is Best Practice 6, Structuring Intentional, Sufficient, and Supported Natural Peer Interactions, because intentional, sufficient, and supported interactions between peers with and without disabilities has been identified as an empirically supported element of effective early childhood inclusive education that educators and care providers need to organize and structure (Barton & Smith, 2015).

The fourth tier of the pyramid focuses upon quality inclusive assessment and instructional practices, which are described in Best Practice 7, Student-Centered, Strength-Based Assessment and Differentiated Instruction; and Best Practice 9, Decision-Making Processes for Determining Where, When, and How to Address IEP Goals for Students with Intensive and Pervasive Support Needs. Both best practices provide guidelines for educators and early childhood care providers to recognize and react responsively to the varying characteristics of the children they serve (Thousand, Villa, & Nevin, 2015). Best Practice 9 specifically outlines ways to address IEP goals, particularly for children with significant and pervasive support needs.

The fifth and top tier of the pyramid articulates the goal of education for young children that is supported by the lower four tiers; namely access to, participation in, and adequate support to succeed in inclusive settings and experiences. Given administrative leadership and support, tools for collaborating, structures for deploying human resources, and strength-based assessment and differentiation of instruction, adults in early childhood education and care settings are poised to attain the ultimate goal of early childhood inclusive education represented by the top tier of the pyramid model. Best Practice 1, Understanding What Inclusive Education Is, details this goal and the defining features of truly inclusive early childhood education.

Figure 1: Early Childhood Inclusive Education Pyramid Model

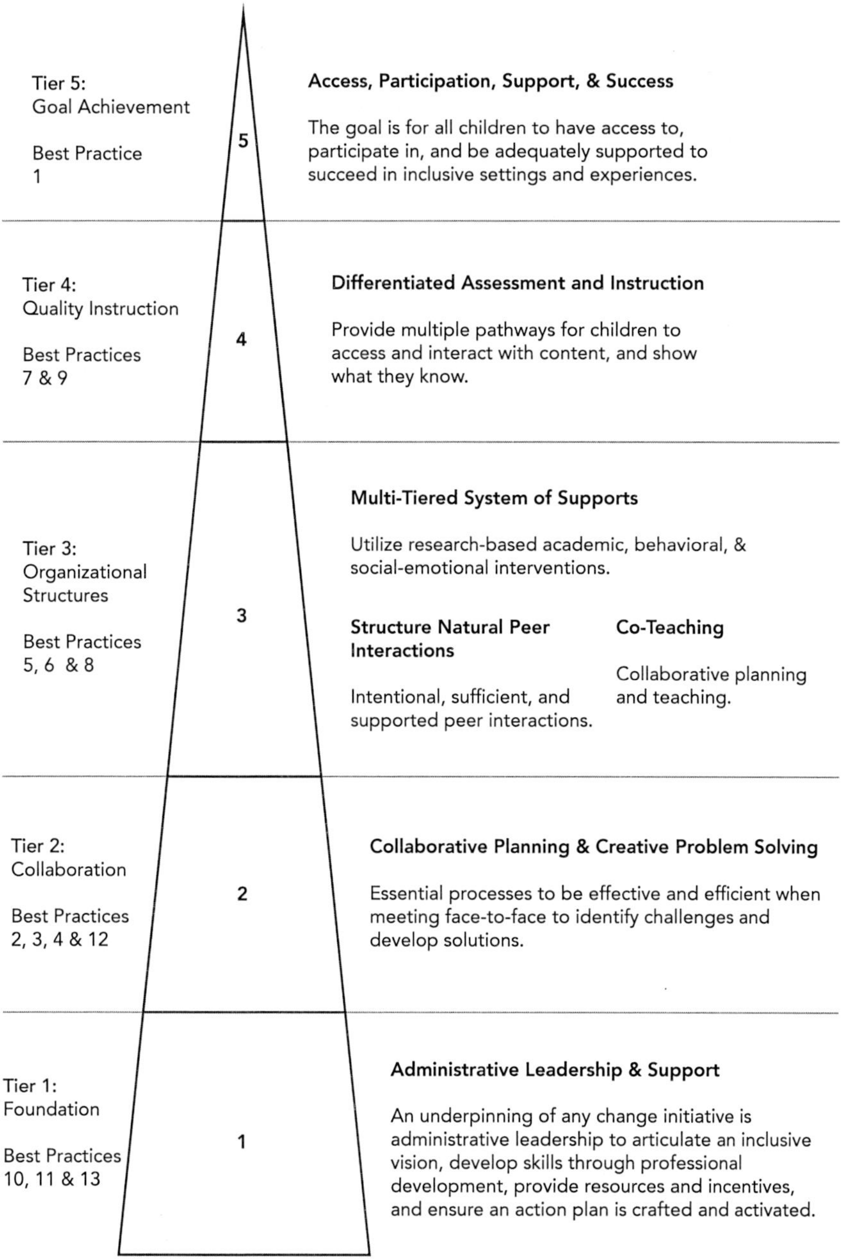

Tier 5: Goal Achievement Best Practice 1	5	**Access, Participation, Support, & Success** The goal is for all children to have access to, participate in, and be adequately supported to succeed in inclusive settings and experiences.
Tier 4: Quality Instruction Best Practices 7 & 9	4	**Differentiated Assessment and Instruction** Provide multiple pathways for children to access and interact with content, and show what they know.
Tier 3: Organizational Structures Best Practices 5, 6 & 8	3	**Multi-Tiered System of Supports** Utilize research-based academic, behavioral, & social-emotional interventions. **Structure Natural Peer Interactions** Intentional, sufficient, and supported peer interactions. **Co-Teaching** Collaborative planning and teaching.
Tier 2: Collaboration Best Practices 2, 3, 4 & 12	2	**Collaborative Planning & Creative Problem Solving** Essential processes to be effective and efficient when meeting face-to-face to identify challenges and develop solutions.
Tier 1: Foundation Best Practices 10, 11 & 13	1	**Administrative Leadership & Support** An underpinning of any change initiative is administrative leadership to articulate an inclusive vision, develop skills through professional development, provide resources and incentives, and ensure an action plan is crafted and activated.

How to Use The Early Childhood Inclusive Education Checklist Self-Assessments

The self-assessments included in the following 13 best practice chapters of *The Early Childhood Inclusive Education Checklist* are designed to assist schools, districts, administrators, policy makers, charter preschool programs, blended early childhood education/ early childhood special education programs, programs operated by public agencies such as Head Start and community-based child care and pre-kindergarten programs, group child development centers, private preschool and child care programs, public and private kindergartens, faith-based programs, recreation programs, and parents and other community members interested in early childhood education with assessing, developing, and implementing inclusive services for young children (ages 3 - 5) with disabilities, and their peers. For each of the 13 best practices, indicator assessment results offer level of implementation data, which can then be used to plan for continuous program improvement.

The structure of Best Practices 1-9 and 11-13 is as follows: First, the best practice is described. Then, a series of 7 to 30 best practice indicators that deconstruct the best practice are listed, with a place for the rater to enter a score in response to the question, "To what degree does this best practice occur in our early childhood education setting(s)?" using the following five-point (i.e., zero to 4) Likert scale and descriptors:

4	3	2	1	0
Always	**Most of the time**	**Some of the time**	**Rarely**	**Never**

Best Practice 10, Professional Learning and Coaching, is structured differently. Given the importance of modeling, guided practice, and coaching in turning theory into practice, following the description of the best practice, the rating scale assesses not only whether professional learning has occurred but the degree to which training on each of the 14 listed topics is supplemented with: (a) live or video modeling and demonstrations; (b) opportunities for participant guided practice; and (c) opportunities for on-site observation, coaching, and performance-based feedback. Thus, the 14 topical indicators for Best Practice 10 are scored using the following 5-point Likert scale.

4	3	2	1	0
On-Site Coaching	**Guided Practice During Training**	**Demonstration & Modeling**	**Lecture & Discussion**	**No Training Opportunity**

Following each set of best practice indicators, a place is provided to enter the total score across items, compute a mean score, and indicate the range (from 0 to 4) of responses. For a 10-item set of best practice indicators, this summary would look as follows:

Total Score (out of 40 maximum): ________

Mean Score (Total Score/10): ________

Range of Scores: ______ **(low) to** _______ **(high)**

The mean score can be computed for an individual respondent, a subgroup of the early childhood learning environments and community partners (e.g., family members, special educators and specialists, related services personnel, caregivers, paraeducators), or aggregated across all respondents. The mean score offers a general indicator of the degree to which elements of a best practice are currently being implemented and can be used as a general indicator of progress toward achieving the best practice.

Using a scale such as the one below, a mean score can be used to signal both the "health" of the general early childhood setting regarding a best practice as well as the degree of need or urgency to work on that best practice. For example, a best practice mean score of 2.0 might suggest that an early childhood setting is "in need of considerable improvement," whereas a mean score of 2.6 might suggest that an early childhood environment is "on its way," yet still in need of considerable improvement.

Progress Toward Early Childhood Inclusive Education Best Practice Excellence
(as Indicated by Mean Score)

3.1 - 4.0	2.1 – 3.0	1.1 – 2.0	0 – 1.0
Doing well	**On our way**	**Need considerable improvement**	**Need to start**

The range of scores data offer another metric that reflects the variability of implementation and quality within a particular best practice area. For example, a mean score of 2.5 might represent a narrow range of scores from 2 to 3 (e.g., representing 5 "most of the time" and 5 "some of the time" scores). A narrower range might suggest the need for a general course of action, such as a professional development and support initiative for all early childhood personnel and their community partners. A mean score of 2.5 could also represent a wide range of scores from 0 to 4 (representing "never" to "always" ratings). A wider range of ratings might suggest the need to target the "never" and "rarely" indicators as priority areas of improvement.

References

Barton, E. E., & Smith, B. J. (2015). *The preschool inclusion toolbox: How to build and lead a high-quality program.* Baltimore, MD: Paul H. Brookes Publishing Co., Inc.

Division of Early Childhood/National Association for the Education of Young Children (DEC/NAEYC). (2009). *Early childhood inclusion: A joint position statement of the Division for Early Childhood (DEC) and the National Association for the Education of Young Children (NAEYC).* Chapel Hill, NC: The University of North Carolina, FPG Child Development Institute.

Strain, P. S., & Smith, L. (2016, February 18). Preschool inclusion: What's the evidence, what gets in the way, and what do high-quality programs look like? [Webinar]. In *2016 National Inclusion Webinar Series of the Early Childhood Technical Assistance Center.* Retrieved from http://ectacenter.org/~calls/2016/nationalinclusion.asp

Thousand, J. S., Villa, R. A., & Nevin, A. I. (2015). *Differentiating instruction: Planning for universal design and teaching for college and career readiness* (2nd ed.). Thousand Oaks, CA: Corwin Press.

Villa, R., & Thousand, J. (2016). *The inclusive education checklist: A self-assessment of best practices.* Naples, FL: National Professional Resources, Inc.

Villa, R., & Thousand, J. (2017). *Leading an inclusive school: Access and success for ALL students.* Alexandria, VA: Association for Supervision and Curriculum Development.

Early Childhood Inclusive Education Best Practice #1:

Understanding What Early Childhood Inclusion Is: Inclusive Early Childhood Education Is a Vision, Policy, and Best Practice

1

We define *inclusive education* for preschool and school-aged children as both the *vision and practice* of welcoming, valuing, empowering, and supporting the diverse academic, social-emotional, language, and communication learning of all students in shared environments and experiences for the purpose of attaining the desired goals of education (Villa & Thousand, 2016). Inclusion is first a *belief* that everyone belongs, regardless of need or perceived ability, and that all are valued and contributing members of the school community. Inclusive education also is the *practice* of differentiating instruction for children through collaborative planning and teaching among all members of a school and learning community, including students and families. It is providing all students with opportunities to experience the goals of education: belonging, mastery, independence (choice making), and generosity (Brendtro, Brokenleg, & Van Bockern, 2009).

In the joint position statement on inclusion ratified by the Division for Early Childhood (DEC) of the Council for Exceptional Children and the National Association for the Education of Young Children (NAEYC) in April of 2009, the DEC and NAEYC further clarify inclusive education as it applies to early childhood education. Like us, these organizations recognize inclusion as both a vision (translated into policy) and a practice. The DEC and NAEYC (2009) position statement defines *early childhood inclusion* as follows:

> Early childhood inclusion embodies the values, policies, and practices that support the right of every infant and young child and his or her family, regardless of ability, to participate in a broad range of activities and contexts as full members of families, communities, and society. The desired results of inclusive experiences for children with and without disabilities and their families include a sense of belonging and membership, positive social relationships and friendships, and development and learning to reach their full potential. The defining features of inclusion that can be used to identify high quality early childhood programs and services are access, participation, and supports. (p. 2)

The position statement continues by defining *access, participation,* and *supports*. *Access* includes a range of learning settings and experiences and can take various forms. Namely, inclusion can occur in "homes, Head Start, child care, faith-based programs, recreational programs, preschool, public and private pre-kindergarten through early elementary education, and blended early childhood education/early childhood special education programs" (DEC/NAEYC, 2009, p. 2). *Participation,* as well as engagement and belonging, is facilitated by adults who intentionally employ a range of supports "—from embedded, routines-based teaching to more explicit interventions—to scaffold learning and participation for all children" (DEC/NAEYC, 2009, p. 2). *Supports* include systems-level infrastructure supports and ongoing professional learning for family members and professionals, as well as resources and policies, including funding policies, for promoting collaboration among groups.

At the federal level, in the "Policy Statement on Inclusion of Children with Disabilities in Early Education Childhood Programs" issued in September of 2015 by the U.S. Department of Health and Human Services and the U.S. Department of Education, the departments endorse and advocate for children with the mildest to the most significant disabilities to be educated with children without disabilities within early childhood programs, in accordance with the Least Restrictive Environment (LRE) requirements articulated in Part B of the federal Individuals with Disabilities Act (IDEA) (2004). The departments define inclusion as "holding high expectations and intentionally promoting participation in all learning and social activities, facilitated by individualized accommodations; and using evidence-based services and supports to foster . . . development (cognitive, language, communication, physical, behavioral, and social-emotional), friendship with peers, and [a] sense of belonging" (U.S. Department of Health and Human Services & U.S. Department of Education, 2015, p. 3).

Inclusive Education Is Presumed Competence

For all students, including students with more extensive support needs (historically referred to as students with moderate and severe disabilities), inclusive education is presuming competence and holding the highest of expectations (National Alternate Assessment Center, 2005) by creating "personally meaningful curriculum" (Bambara, Koger, Burns, & Singley, 2016, p. 475) that blends opportunities to acquire academic and functional knowledge and skills within the context of general education and natural routines, "with decisions about 'what to teach when and where' driven by family and individual preferences, values, and vision" (Bambara et al., 2016, p. 475).

Biklen and Burke (2006) recognize a "tradition in American education to assume incompetence of students who have severe communication impairments . . . through the process of classification" (p. 166). They point out that each of us has a choice to presume a person with significant disabilities to be incompetent, or "admit that one cannot know another's thinking unless the other can reveal it. The latter . . . more conservative choice . . . refuses to limit opportunity by presuming competence" (p. 166). Presumption of competence in the absence of evidence to the contrary is not a new notion. In the early 1980s, Donnellan and Leary (1984) described the notion of presumed competence, naming it the *criterion of least dangerous assumption.*

Summarizing, Jorgensen (2005) writes, "the least-dangerous assumption when working with students with significant disabilities is to assume that they are competent and able to learn, because to do otherwise would result in harm such as fewer educational opportunities, inferior literacy instruction, a segregated education, and fewer choices as an adult" (p. 5). The most dangerous assumption is to fail to presume competence, intelligence, and potential for growth. The criterion of least dangerous assumption is the *presumption of competence at all times for all persons.*

Inclusion in Early Childhood Education Is Supported by Research

> "It is well documented that the beginning years of all children's lives are critical for building the early foundations of learning and wellness needed for success in school and later in life."
>
> —U.S. Department of Health and Human Services & U.S. Department of Education (2015)

As early as the 1980s, research showed that, for school-aged children, separate special education services had little to no positive effects for students, regardless of the intensity or type of their disabilities (Lipsky & Gartner, 1989). In a meta-analysis of effective special education settings, Baker, Wang, and Wahlberg (1994) concluded that for school-aged children, "special-needs students educated in regular classes do better academically and socially than comparable students in non-inclusive settings" (p. 34). This held true regardless of the type of disability or grade level of the student. As for the impact of inclusive educational experiences prior to exiting public school, over 20 years ago the U.S. Department of Education reported that "across a number of analyses of post-school results, the message was the same: those who spent more time in regular education experienced better results after high school" (1995, p. 87).

The research regarding the effect of inclusive early childhood education experiences of preschoolers with identified disabilities reflects and expands upon the positive outcomes found for school-aged students. Summarizing inclusive early education research in a Strain and Smith (2016) webinar, Dr. Phil Strain notes the following five general findings:

1. *Student learning is superior in inclusive settings.* "High quality inclusive settings are the only environments . . . with data that consistently support children's superior learning. And importantly, there have been a number of well controlled experimental studies in which children in non-inclusive settings have been shown to have their learning negatively impacted. That is to say, after being taught certain social and language skills, subsequent placement in settings with only other similarly disabled children has resulted in rapid skill loss" (Strain & Smith, 2016). Early childhood research that contributes to this general finding include Rafferty, Piscitelli, and Boettcher's 2003 study on the positive impact of preschool inclusion on the language development of children with significant and pervasive support needs, and Strain and Hoyson's 2000 longitudinal study on the positive long-term impact of inclusive preschool experiences on multiple dimensions of development for children with autism.

2. *Quality inclusive education differentiated based upon student support needs yields positive outcomes across the range of disability categories, varying intensity of support needs, and type of inclusive setting.* "The data on inclusion comes from children with mild to severe developmental delays, children on the autism spectrum, children with multiple disabilities, children with significant social and emotional needs, children with hearing impairment, and children with limited mobility . . . [and] from childcare settings, from head start, from public pre-k, and from private pre-k . . . Some of the most powerful outcomes that have been reported in the literature come from children who have some of the most significant developmental needs. As it turns out, the data don't support the common perception that children who are less involved are better candidates for inclusion. . . . [And] quality inclusion will look real

different for different groups of children and different children within groups" (Strain & Smith, 2016). See, for example, outcomes reported by Rafferty and colleagues (2003) and Strain and Hoyson (2000) in the previous paragraph.

3. *Inclusive settings provide higher quality learning experiences.* "Compar[ing] inclusionary settings to non-inclusionary settings . . . , inclusionary settings tend to be programs that are more evidence based in their selection and use of instructional practices . . . , maximize families' involvement, and . . . [are] more data driven in their approach to the provision of special education and related services" (Strain & Smith, 2016). Early childhood research that contributes to this general finding includes studies by Grisham-Brown, Pretti-Frontczak, Hawkins and Winchell (2009), and Rakap and Parlak-Rakap (2011) that demonstrate the effectiveness and efficiency of embedding intensive instruction in daily activities of inclusive early childhood programs. Buysse, Wesley, Bryant, and Gardner (1999) also found that early childhood programs that included at least one child with disabilities scored significantly higher on measures of program quality.

4. *Although communication and cognitive skill development are greater in inclusive settings, the greatest growth gains are in the social domain.* "There have been to date about 40 years of research . . . in which people have asked the question, 'What's the long-term impact on developing friendships, being a part of a friendship network when you're a preschooler and what happens later in life?' In fact . . . , it's possible to argue with confidence that these are some of the most reliable data in all of the behavioral sciences because there's no . . . data to the contrary" (Strain & Smith, 2016). Early childhood research that contributes to this general finding includes Holahan and Costenbader's (2000) findings that children with disabilities in inclusive early childhood programs demonstrated stronger social-emotional skills than those educated in separate, non-inclusive settings.

Buysse, Goldman, and Skinner (2002) found that children with disabilities in inclusive settings developed friendships with typically developing peers. Cross, Traub, Hutter-Pishgahi, and Shelton's 2004 examination of peers of children with disabilities in inclusive classrooms found peers to be helpful and learning to be compassionate and empathetic, as reported by parents and teachers.

5. *The data favoring inclusive education is overwhelming.* "If you simply look at the number of studies that have been published in peer reviewed journals directly comparing comparable children in inclusive and non-inclusive settings, the ratio with which inclusive settings beat the alternative is about 15 to 1" (Strain & Smith, 2016). This finding reinforces and extends the 2004 IDEA reauthorization's finding that "almost 30 years of research and experience has demonstrated that the education of children with disabilities can be made more effective by: a) having high expectations for such children and ensuring their access in the general education curriculum in the regular classroom, to the maximum extent possible . . . [and] providing appropriate special education and related services, and aides and supports in the regular classroom, to such children, whenever appropriate" (20 U.S.C. 1400(c)(5)).

In addition to these five general findings, Barton and Smith (2015) note findings as to the benefits of inclusion for children without disabilities; the cost effectiveness of inclusive programs (i.e., inclusive programs are no more expensive than separate programs); and the influence parent and teacher attitudes about disability can have on the attitudes of typically developing preschoolers regarding their peers with disabilities.

In summary, the data speak volumes in support of early childhood inclusion: all children, including preschoolers with a broad range of disabilities, can experience greater learning, language, and social outcomes in inclusive settings.

Inclusion Is a Journey

In an *OSEP Dear Colleague Letter on Preschool (LRE),* Melody Musgrove, the then-Director of the Office of Special Education Programs (OSEP), affirmed that the least restrictive environment (LRE) requirements of IDEA do indeed apply to preschoolers aged three through five with disabilities, as the "provision on LRE does not distinguish between school-aged and preschool-aged children and, therefore, applies equally to all preschool children with disabilities" (Musgrove, 2012). The letter summarizes the LRE requirements as follows:

> These requirements state the IDEA's strong preference for educating students with disabilities in regular classes with appropriate aids and supports. . . . [and that], to the maximum extent appropriate, children with disabilities, including children in public or private institutions or other care facilities, must be educated with children who are not disabled. Further, special classes, separate schooling, or other removal of children with disabilities from the regular education environment may occur only when the nature or severity of the disability of a child is such that education in regular classes with the use of supplementary aides and services cannot be achieved satisfactorily. (Musgrove, 2012)

Ideally, the goal of inclusive education is for nearly 100% of children with disabilities to be educated within inclusive educational settings with nondisabled peers nearly 100% of their educational day.

As reported in the U.S. Department of Education's 2017 annual report to Congress for the year 2015, nationally, only 43.8% of pre-k children covered under Part B of IDEA (i.e., children ages three through five not yet attending kindergarten) were educated with nondisabled peers. Further, given that 30 years prior, 36.8% of pre-k children with IEPs were served in inclusive settings (U.S. Department of Education, 1987), the current percentage represents a mere 7% increase over 30 years in the proportion of special education-eligible pre-k children served in inclusive settings.

In contrast, the U.S. Department of Education's 2017 annual report to Congress reports that for the year 2015, 62.7% of school-aged students were educated with nondisabled peers for 80% or more of the day—nearly 19% more than pre-k children.[1] Further, in 1985 just under 25% of school-aged children with disabilities were educated primarily in general education (Hume, 1988), revealing an increase of approximately 33% in inclusive placements over a 30-year period, versus an increase of only 7% in that same period for pre-k children.

The pre-k and school-aged data suggest that most communities and school districts have a distance to go in their journey to achieving the ideal. Why? As Barton and Smith (2015) aptly state, "[i]nclusion at the pre-k level presents a unique set of challenges. Unlike K-12 education, which is available to all students through the public schools, districts might not have inclusive preschool classrooms" (p. 155).

Musgrove (2012) and Barton and Smith (2015) identify some inclusive alternatives for educating preschoolers with disabilities. In addition to public preschool programs for children without disabilities offered by a school district or charter school and blended early childhood education/early childhood special education programs, alternatives include, but are not limited to, programs operated by public agencies such as Head Start and community-based child care and pre-kindergarten programs, group child development centers, private preschool and child care programs, public and private kindergartens, faith-based programs, and recreation programs. It is noted that, "[if] a public agency determines that placement in a private preschool program is necessary for a child to receive FAPE, the public agency must make that program available at no cost to the parent" (Musgrove, 2012).

---

[1] The U.S. Department of Health and Human Services and the U.S. Department of Education (2015) define early childhood programs as those that provide early care and education to children birth through age five, where the majority of children in the program are typically developing. For federal data collection purposes, for an early childhood program to be considered inclusive or a "regular" program, the majority (50% or more) of the children attending must be nondisabled (Musgrove, 2012).

Why else do many communities and school districts still have a distance to go in their journey to achieve inclusive educational opportunities for preschoolers with disabilities? Some school systems have yet to attempt or achieve consensus on an inclusive vision for students with disabilities of any age. Some schools have yet to orchestrate structural supports (e.g., co-teaching and otherwise blending or braiding of the instructional and financial resources of public and private agencies and programs within the community) to make it happen easily. Some schools have yet to provide their school personnel with professional learning and coaching opportunities in how to meet diverse student needs in mixed-ability student groupings and classrooms. Finally, there are those few students (e.g., students who are hospitalized) for whom being educated within an inclusive setting does not best support their momentary needs or goals. It is for these reasons that we do not identify 100% as the target for the best practices Indicator 1.

Indicator 1 targets at least 80% (rather than 43.8%) of three to five-year old students with IEPs having inclusive community or school settings as a primary educational placement. Why set a target of 80%, which is nearly double the national average of 43.8%? Because national averages are just that, a central tendency measure representing communities performing both below and above the mean. Averages factor in the fact that there are states, districts, and communities across the nation that do exceed the mean. Since this is a best practice indicator, we chose a target that substantially exceeds the national average, yet is within reach. Recall that the recent national average of school-aged students being educated with nondisabled peers (i.e., 62.7%) already more closely approximates an 80% target. An 80% target can create a sense of urgency for districts to set goals for preschool inclusion that move toward this target and to take decisive action to achieve their interim goals.

For federal data collection purposes, for an early childhood program to be considered inclusive or a "regular" program, the majority (50% or more) of the children attending must be non-disabled (Musgrove, 2012). Note that Indicator 2 suggests that for an early childhood program to be considered a high quality inclusive program, the proportion of children without disabilities in attendance should be considerably more than 50% (i.e., 66% to 75%). Dr. Phil Strain articulates why:

> So what characterizes these high quality programs? One of the things that characterizes the programs is that they have more typically developing children than children with special needs enrolled. Some of the best data on the topic come from my friends. The three of us—Elieen Schwartz, Gayle McGee and I—have all been studying problems and potentials around inclusion for at least 30 years. And it's instructive, I think, that we all began with a 50/50 ratio . . . However, over time, we abandoned that 50/50 ratio for good reasons, and at a minimum we've gone now to a 2 or a 3 to 1 ratio. What that has done for us is that it's provided far more generalization opportunities in that all important peer social domain. That is to say, children with special needs have more play partners, more varied interaction, more opportunity to practice their peer-related social skills. (Strain & Smith, 2016)

A two to one ratio would mean that at least two out of three or 66.6% of students attending a quality inclusive early childhood program would not have an identified disability; a three to one ratio translates into three out of four or 75% of students not having a disability. Because of this research-based recommendation, for Indicator 2, we set as a target just over a two to one non-disabled to disabled student ratio. In other words, we suggest that for an early childhood setting to be considered a high quality inclusive early childhood setting, at least two thirds or 67% of students enrolled would NOT have identified disabilities.

We anticipate that the target percentages for this and other indicators should and will rise over time. As we do better, we can set our sights higher—on even more ambitious targets. It is our hope that the use of this best practice assessment tool and its indicators will hasten the day when the ideal becomes the reality for all preschoolers with disabilities, their families, and the educators and other support personnel responsible for their education.

Early Childhood Inclusive Education Best Practice Checklist Assessment

Best Practice #1: *Understanding What Early Childhood Inclusion Is*

Directions: Based upon your experience, please give each of the 12 indicators a (zero to 4) rating in response to the question, "To what degree does this best practice occur in our early childhood education setting(s)?"

4	3	2	1	0
Always	**Most of the time**	**Some of the time**	**Rarely**	**Never**

Rating (0 – 4)	Indicator of Understanding What Early Childhood Inclusion Is
☐	1. Across all ethnic, racial, primary language, and special education eligibility categories, *at least 80%* of children with disabilities ages three through five are *educated in inclusive early childhood settings* and programs, which include, but are not limited to, public and charter preschool programs for children without disabilities, blended early childhood education/early childhood special education programs, programs operated by public agencies such as Head Start and community-based child care and pre-kindergarten programs, group child development centers, private preschool and child care programs, public and private kindergartens, faith-based programs, and recreation programs. This applies to all young children with disabilities, from those with the mildest to the most significant disabilities. (See the explanation for this target percentage in the "Inclusive Education is a Journey" section of the preceding narrative.)

Rating (0 - 4)	Indicator of Understanding What Early Childhood Inclusion Is
☐	2. At least *two thirds or 67%* of students enrolled in inclusive early childhood settings and programs in which children with disabilities ages three through five receive special education services *do NOT have identified disabilities.* (See the explanation for this target percentage in the "Inclusive Education is a Journey" section of the preceding narrative.)
☐	3. The population of students enrolled in inclusive early childhood programs in which children with disabilities ages three through five receive special education services *proportionately represents* the *ethnic, racial, socio-economic, and linguistic diversity of the community* in which the program is provided.
☐	4. Each child with a disability ages three through five is *included several days per week* in social and learning opportunities with typical peers.
☐	5. For each child, *placement decisions* are based upon the *individual needs* of the child and consideration of *family preferences* as agreed on in the IEP.
☐	6. The *placement option of first choice* discussed for each child with a disability ages three through five is in an *inclusive early childhood setting* (i.e., one that includes nondisabled peers) with the provision of necessary and effective special education and related supplemental *supports, aids, and services.* The presumption is that the student is educated with his/her non-disabled peers with the provision of specially designed instruction (special education services, supplementary aids and services, and related services).

[2] In their review of over a quarter century of research on early childhood education and outcomes for preschoolers with disabilities, Strain, Bovey, Wilson and Royball (2009) found that inclusive services produce benefits for children with disabilities only when young children are included several days per week in social and learning opportunities with typical peers.

Rating (0 – 4)	Indicator of Understanding What Early Childhood Inclusion Is
☐	7. Children with disabilities ages three through five have *access* to the *same activities* as their non-disabled peers. (Note: The IDEA defines curriculum as the sum total of all experiences inclusive of co-curricular activities made available to nondisabled students.)
☐	8. Person first language is used when describing students. When describing a student, ability is emphasized (e.g., "uses a communication device" rather than "unable to speak"); and the person is put first, before the disability (e.g., "a child with ADHD" rather than "the ADHD kid"). We do not refer to students by categorical labels or program name (e.g., special class students, sped kid, ELLs).
☐	9. Personnel serving children with disabilities ages three through five (e.g., child care providers, special and general educators, related service personnel, paraeducators, administrators,) *presume competence* for all students and especially students with difficulties in communicating and those with significant and pervasive support needs. (Please see the "Inclusive Education is Presumed Competence" section in the preceding narrative for the meaning of presumed competence as used in this indicator.)
☐	10. Personnel working in inclusive early childhood education settings serving preschoolers with disabilities are provided with and use specific *information regarding* each student's *strengths* (e.g., learning preferences) and *needs* (e.g., social-emotional, communication, language goals) in order to facilitate and support each student's *development*.

Rating (0 – 4)	Indicator of Understanding What Early Childhood Inclusion Is
☐	11. Lack of *resources, adequate personnel, or adequate personnel preparation* is NOT used to argue that a student with a disability should be excluded or removed from an inclusive early childhood educational setting.
☐	12. The *need for modifications* to the early childhood curriculum is NOT used to argue that a student with a disability should be excluded or removed from an inclusive early childhood educational setting.

Total Score (out of 48 maximum): ________

Mean Score (Total Score/12): ________

Range of Scores: ______ **(low) to** ______ **(high)**

References

Baker, E. T., Wang, M. C., (1994). The effects of inclusion on learning. *Educational Leadership, 52*(4), 33-35.

Bambara, L. M., Koger, F., Burns, R. & Singley, D. (2016). Building skills for home and community. In F. Brown, J. McDonnell, & M. E. Snell (Eds.), *Education students with severe disabilities* (8th ed.) (pp. 438-473). Boston: Pearson.

Barton, E. E., & Smith, B. J. (2015). *The preschool inclusion toolbox: How to build and lead a high-quality program.* Baltimore, MD: Paul H. Brookes Publishing Co., Inc.

Brendtro, L. K., Brokenleg, M., & Van Bockern. S. (2009). *Reclaiming youth at risk: Our hope for the future (Rev. Ed.).* Bloomington, IN: Solution Tree Press.

Buysse, V., Goldman, B. D., & Skinner, M. L. (2002). Setting effects on friendship formation among young children with and without disabilities. *Exceptional Children, 68,* 503-517.

Buysse, V., Wesley, P. W., Bryant, D. M., & Gardner, D. (1999). Quality of early childhood programs in inclusive and noninclusive settings. *Exceptional Children, 65,* 301-314.

Cross, A. F., Traub, E. K., Hutter-Pishgahi, L., & Shelton, G. (2004). Elements for successful inclusion of children with significant disabilities. *Topics in Early Childhood Special Education, 24,* 169-183.

Danaher, J. (2005). *Eligibility policies and practices for young children under Part B of IDEA.* Chapel Hill, NC: The National Early Childhood Technical Assistance Center of The University of North Carolina at Chapel Hill, FPG Development Institute.

Division of Early Childhood/National Association for the Education of Young Children (DEC/NAEYC). (2009). *Early childhood inclusion: A joint position statement of the Division for Early Childhood (DEC) and the National Association for the Education of Young Children (NAEYC).* Chapel Hill, NC: The University of North Carolina, FPG Child Development Institute.

Donnellan, A. M., & Leary, M. R. (1984). *Movement differences and diversity in autism/mental retardation: Appreciating and accommodating people with communication and behavior challenges.* Madison, WI: DRI Press.

Grisham-Brown, J., Pretti-Frontczak, K., Hawkins, S. R., & Winchell, B. N. (2009). Addressing early learning standards for all children within blended preschool classrooms. *Topics in Early Childhood Education, 29,* 131-142.

Holahan, A., & Costenbader, V. (2000). A comparison of developmental gains for preschool children with disabilities in inclusive and self-contained classrooms. *Topics in Early Childhood Special Education, 20,* 224-235.

Hume, M. (1998, March 4). Another year increases the demand on special education, report shows. *Education Daily,* 7-8.

Individuals with Disabilities Education Act (IDEA), 20 U.S.C. §1400 (2004).

Jorgensen, C. (2005). The least dangerous assumption: A challenge to create a new paradigm. *Disability Solutions, 6*(6), 24-29.

Lipskey, D. K.; & Gartner, A. (1989). *Beyond separate education: Quality education for all.* Baltimore, MD: Paul H. Brookes Publishing Co., Inc.

Musgrove, M. (2012, February 29). *OSEP dear colleague letter on preschool (LRER).* Retrieved from www2.ed.gov/policy/speced/guid/idea/memosdcltrs/preschoollre22912.doc

National Alternate Assessment Center. *(2005). Designing from the ground floor: Alternate assessment on alternate achievement standards.* Session presented at the Council of Chief State School Officer's Annual Large Scale Assessment Conference. June 19-22, 2005, San Antonio, TX.

Rafferty, Y., Piscitelli, V., & Boettcher, C. (2003). The impact of inclusion on language development and social competence among preschoolers with disabilities. *Exceptional Children, 69,* 467-479.

Rakap, S., & Parlak-Rakap, A. (2011). Effectiveness of embedded instruction in early childhood special education: A literature review. *European Early Childhood Education Research Journal, 19,* 79-96.

Strain, P. S., & Bovey, E. H., Wilson, K., & Royball, R. (2009). LEEP preschool: Lessons learned over 28 years of inclusive services for young children with autism. *Young Exceptional Children Monograph Series No. 11,* 49-68.

Strain, P. S., & Bovey, E. H. (2011). Randomized, controlled trial of the LEAP model of early intervention for young children with Autism Spectrum Disorders. *Topics in Early Childhood Special Education, 31,* 133-154.

Strain, P. S., & Hoyson, M. (2000). The need for longitudinal intensive social skill intervention: LEAP follow-up outcomes for children with autism. *Topics in Early Childhood Special Education, 20,* 116-122.

Strain, P. S., & Smith, L. (2016, February 18). Preschool inclusion: What's the evidence, what gets in the way, and what do high-quality programs look like? [Webinar]. In *2016 National Inclusion Webinar Series of the Early Childhood Technical Assistance Center.* Retrieved from http://ectacenter.org/~calls/2016/nationalinclusion.asp

Thousand, J. S., Villa, R. A., & Nevin, A. I. (2015). *Differentiating instruction: Planning for universal design and teaching for college and career readiness* (2nd ed.). Thousand Oaks, CA: Corwin Press.

U.S. Department of Education. (1987). *Annual report to congress on the implementation of the Individuals with Disabilities Education Act.* Washington, DC: Author.

U.S. Depatment of Education (1995). *Seventeenth annual report to Congress on the implemenataion of the Individuals with Disabilties Act.* Washington, D.C.: Author.

U.S. Department of Education. (2017). *39th annual report to congress on the implementation of the Individuals with Disabilities Education Act, 2017.* Washington, DC: Author.

U.S. Department of Health and Human Services & U.S. Department of Education. (2015, September 14). *Policy statement on inclusion of children with disabilities in early childhood programs.* Washington, DC: Authors. Retrieved from www2.ed.gov/policy/speced/guid/earlylearning/joint-statement-full-text.pdf

Villa, R., & Thousand, J. (2016). *The inclusive education checklist: A self-assessment of best practices.* Naples, FL: National Professional Resources, Inc.

Villa, R., & Thousand, J. (2017). *Leading an inclusive school: Access and success for ALL students.* Alexandria, VA: Association for Supervision and Curriculum Development.

2 Early Childhood Inclusive Education Best Practice #2: *Home-School-Community Collaboration*

Family members are the first and most important teachers and advocates of young children. The importance of parent and family engagement has been long documented (National Center on Educational Restructuring and Inclusion, 1995). The U.S. Congress recognized the power of parent participation in the findings of the 2004 reauthorization of the Individuals with Disabilities Education Act (IDEA), acknowledging that, "nearly 30 years of research and experience has demonstrated that the education of children with disabilities can be made more effective by . . . strengthening the role of parents and ensuring that families of such children have meaningful opportunities to participate in the education of their children - at school and at home" (20 U.S.C. § 1401(c)(5)(b)).

Families are the building blocks of society and the constant in the lives of their sons and daughters. Therefore, educators are obliged to provide opportunities for families to participate as integral partners in the development, implementation, and evaluation of the success of their children's Individual Education Programs (IEPs). Educators and students can only benefit from doing everything possible to facilitate *home-school collaboration.* Active engagement of family members in the IEP process is one of the best ways to ensure that a child's goals are implemented, not only at the site(s) where a child is receiving education services, but at home and in the community. Such engagement assumes and requires that professionals working with and for families are deliberate in learning about and *using* what they learn about each family's cultural, linguistic, and other dimensions of diversity to plan for each child's educational program. In other words, effective home-school collaboration relies upon the professionals working for and with families to learn to be and act as culturally competent as possible (Lindsey, Thousand, Jew, & Piowlski, 2018).

Schools and other programs and agencies supporting young children with IEPs, as well as students and families, benefit from *school-community collaborations.* As we already have learned (in Chapter 1), many of the inclusive educational settings that can and do serve young children with IEPs (e.g., community-based child care and pre-kindergarten programs; child development centers; private preschool, child care, and kindergartens) are community- rather than school-based. Further, young children may receive care and education from multiple home, community, and school-based providers across a single day or week. Given the many people who may interact with a child across various environments, in order to optimize opportunities for teaching and reinforcing a child's learning across settings, it is essential that important information (e.g., needed behavior supports, effective instructional strategies and supports, emerging communication system) be exchanged in planful ways among personnel of all settings.

Schools not only can partner with community agencies that typically provide services to children and families, but they can also expand the potential services available to children and create opportunities for family members to become involved in community and school activities by establishing partnerships with private foundations, volunteer organizations, YMCAs and other youth and recreational organizations, university teacher preparation programs, and other service-oriented organizations. Additionally, schools should take the lead in communicating and collaborating with personnel of community settings and programs in which the children they serve participate. By taking the lead, schools ensure personnel across settings have a clear understanding of each child's IEP goals and needed supports and services, and set the stage for providing training, modeling, and coaching, as needed, to facilitate each child's participation and success in these other settings.

The IDEA requires that IEP teams make service and setting decisions for young children with disabilities based upon their individual needs (U.S. Department of Health and Human Services & U.S. Department of Education, 2015). Local Education Agencies (LEAs) and schools, therefore, have a responsibility to take the lead to establish partnerships and formal agreements with early childhood education programs and service providers in the community, and facilitate communication among school personnel, community partners, and families.

In summary, when all parties have clear understandings of their roles and responsibilities for ensuring alignment and delivery of comprehensive services to young children with and without disabilities, home-school-community collaboration can be a win-win proposition for all involved.

Early Childhood Inclusive Education Best Practice Checklist Assessment

Best Practice #2: *Home-School-Community Collaboration*

Directions: Based upon your experience, please give each of the 19 indicators a (zero to 4) rating in response to the question, "To what degree does this best practice occur in our early childhood education setting(s)?"

4	3	2	1	0
Always	**Most of the time**	**Some of the time**	**Rarely**	**Never**

Rating (0 – 4)	Indicator of Home-School-Community Collaboration
☐	1. The school district and community programs providing special education and early childhood services to children with disabilities ages three through five provide family members (e.g., parents, guardians) with information in accessible formats (e.g., in the family's primary language) to understand how to *navigate the systems* that serve their children.
☐	2. Parents (or guardians) are: a) *informed of their due process and procedural safeguards and their rights* regarding confidentiality of student records, b) provided *clear information* about whom to contact and what steps to take when they have an educational concern, and c) offered *ready access* to records they seek in accessible formats and in a manner consistent with district policies and procedures.
☐	3. All personnel serving a young child with an IEP *maintain confidentiality* with respect to information about students with IEPs and their families. Only personnel with a legitimate interest in the education of

Rating (0 – 4)	Indicator of Home-School-Community Collaboration
	a student with an IEP have access to that student's records.
☐	4. The school district and community programs providing special education and early childhood services to children with disabilities ages three through five inform family members (e.g., parents, guardians) about *inclusive educational options* and the short- and long-term benefits of inclusive educational experiences.
☐	5. Educational and other service personnel are deliberate about *learning about and using* what they learn about each family's cultural, linguistic, and other dimensions of diversity in interacting with and planning for a child's educational program.
☐	6. Educational and service personnel of other agencies or programs serving a child intentionally *engage and collaborate* with family members in the assessment, IEP goal writing, intervention, and evaluation processes for their child.
☐	7. When making IEP-related decisions, educational and other service personnel *solicit and consider family members'* perspectives regarding their child's strengths, interests, and learning preferences, and incorporate the family's culture, preferences, and priorities into their child's goals and learning experiences using family-driven, person-centered processes (see Chapter 7 for MAPs and Pathways processes).
☐	8. Family members are encouraged to *invite to meetings* regarding their child any individuals (friend, another parent of a child with a disability, advocate, sibling) whom they would like to attend.
☐	9. Programs serving young children with IEPs and their families provide the parents and family members of

Rating (0 – 4)	Indicator of Home-School-Community Collaboration
	each child with opportunities to *develop their knowledge and skills* to support and advance the development and well-being of their child.
☐	10. Programs serving young children with IEPs have *structures and procedures* (e.g., holding meetings at times when family members can attend, home visits) that facilitate communication between families and service providers, not only at IEP planning meetings, but on an on-going basis throughout the year.
☐	11. Families of young children with IEPs have frequent opportunities to *visit the educational settings* in which their children are being served.
☐	12. Families of young children with IEPs are *included in all invitations* to functions and volunteer/service opportunities of the programs serving their children.
☐	13. When policies and procedures regarding special education services are updated, *input is solicited* from family members and community partners as well as staff.
☐	14. Early childhood programs serving children with IEPs have a *designated position* for a family member of a child with an IEP on parent-teacher associations, site improvement councils, and other similar decision-making and advisory groups.
☐	15. Local Education Agencies (LEAs) and schools take the lead in initiating and *establishing partnerships* and formal agreements with early childhood education programs and service providers in the community, and facilitating communication among school personnel, community partners, and families.
☐	16. For each young child with an IEP receiving special education services, the special educators and other specialized personnel serving that child *communicate*

Rating (0 – 4)	Indicator of Home-School-Community Collaboration
	and *collaborate* with the caregivers and educators of the other community setting(s) and program(s) in which the child participates to: a) ensure knowledge and understanding of the child's IEP goals and needed supports and services; and b) provide training, modeling, and coaching, as needed, to facilitate the child's participation and success in the(se) other setting(s).
☐	17. Early childhood programs serving young children with IEPs collaborate with a variety of *community partners* (e.g., child care and other community agencies that serve young children, private foundations, volunteer organizations, recreational youth organizations, local disability support groups, universities, service-oriented organizations) to expand community resources and services to meet school and student needs.
☐	18. The school district *connects families* of young children with IEPs *with state and community resources* (e.g., Parent Training and Information Network, family health resource centers, the state disability rights and legal assistance organization) and partnerships relevant to each family's support interests and needs.
☐	19. The school district and early childhood community partner programs have established *formal agreements* regarding roles and responsibilities for ensuring alignment and delivery of comprehensive services to young children with and without disabilities in inclusive environments.

Total Score (out of 76 maximum): ________

Mean Score (Total Score/19): ________

Range of Scores: ______ **(low) to** ______ **(high)**

References

Individuals with Disabilities Education Act (IDEA), 20 U.S.C. §1400 (2004).

Lindsey, D. B., Thousand, J. S., Jew, C. L., & Piowlski, L. R. (2018). *Culturally proficient inclusive schools: All means ALL!* Thousand Oaks, CA: Corwin Press.

National Center for Educational Restructuring and Inclusion (1995). *National study on inclusive education.* New York: City University of New York. Retrieved from https://eric.ed.gov/?id=ED375606

U.S. Department of Health and Human Services & U.S. Department of Education. (2015, September 14). *Policy statement on inclusion of children with disabilities in early childhood programs.* Washington, D.C.: Authors. Retrieved from www2.ed.gov/policy/speced/guid/earlylearning/joint-statement-full-text.pdf

Early Childhood Inclusive Education Best Practice Checklist Assessment

Best Practice #3:
Redefined Roles And Responsibilities of Early Childhood Care Providers and Educators, Special Educators, Related Services Personnel and Other Support and Health Specialists, and Paraeducators

Directions: Based upon your experience, please give each of the 30 indicators a (zero to 4) rating in response to the question, "To what degree does this best practice occur in our early childhood education setting(s)?"

4	3	2	1	0
Always	Most of the time	Some of the time	Rarely	Never

Rating (0 - 4) | **Indicator of Redefined Roles And Responsibilities of Early Childhood Care Providers and Educators, Special Educators, Related Services Personnel and Other Support/Health Specialists, and Paraeducators**

TO BE COMPLETED BY EARLY CHILDHOOD CARE PROVIDERS AND EDUCATORS (including volunteers)
Directions for rating: Please rate each item using the following sentence starter: *"In our inclusive early childhood education environments, early childhood educators . . . "*

☐ 1. *have ownership for,* and *assume primary responsibility for EVERY student,* including students with disabilities.

☐ 2. *actively participate in IEP meetings* for students with disabilities and other students who struggle in learning.

☐ 3. actively participate with special education teachers, related services personnel (e.g., speech and language pathologist), and other support and health specialists to *collaboratively plan for differentiated instruction and collaboratively evaluate* student progress.

Rating (0 – 4)	Indicator of Redefined Roles And Responsibilities of Early Childhood Care Providers and Educators, Special Educators, Related Services Personnel and Other Support/Health Specialists, and Paraeducators
☐	4. work collaboratively with special educators and others to *identify and implement specific curricular adaptations and instructional strategies* needed by students with disabilities and other students who struggle in learning.
☐	5. work with others to *train and supervise paraeducators* to provide learning support to students with disabilities and other students who struggle in learning.
☐	6. *co-teach* with special educators and other support and health specialists to facilitate student access to the content being taught.
☐	7. *use evidence-based practices* such as natural peer supports, cooperative and partner learning structures, nonlinguistic representations, and differentiated instruction to support meaningful inclusive experiences.
☐	8. actively facilitate *positive social relationships* among students with and without disabilities in social and learning experiences.
☐	9. work collaboratively with others to *keep parents regularly informed of student progress*, including the progress of students with disabilities on IEP and other general curriculum goals.

Rating (0 – 4) **Indicator of Redefined Roles And Responsibilities of Early Childhood Care Providers and Educators, Special Educators, Related Services Personnel and Other Support/Health Specialists, and Paraeducators**

TO BE COMPLETED BY SPECIAL EDUCATORS, RELATED SERVICES PERSONNEL, AND OTHER SUPPORT AND HEALTH SPECIALISTS

Special Note: Rather than scoring each role separately, provide a rating that best represents how specialists *typically* practice their roles in your inclusive early childhood setting.

Directions for rating: Please rate each item using the following sentence starter: *"In our inclusive early childhood education environments, special educators and other support and health specialists . . . "*

☐ 10. *schedule, actively participate in, and facilitate* meetings for students with disabilities and students who otherwise need differentiated learning, communication, behavior, and/or social-emotional support.

☐ 11. actively collaborate with early childhood educators and others to *collect and interpret assessment data to track progress in the curriculum and toward IEP goal attainment* for students with disabilities.

☐ 12. work collaboratively with others to ensure that *IEP goals are addressed in students' daily schedules.*

☐ 13. work collaboratively with early childhood educators and others to *identify and implement specific curricular adaptations and instructional strategies* needed by students with disabilities and other students who are struggling.

☐ 14. provide *professional development* to early childhood providers and educators in topics such as child development, early childhood pedagogy, individualization of instruction, positive behavior supports, and the promotion of social-emotional learning in order to enhance their knowledge and competencies to effectively include young children with disabilities in their settings and programs.

Rating (0 – 4)	Indicator of Redefined Roles And Responsibilities of Early Childhood Care Providers and Educators, Special Educators, Related Services Personnel and Other Support/Health Specialists, and Paraeducators
☐	15. *model* for early childhood educators, paraeducators, and other support personnel methods and strategies for supporting students with disabilities in inclusive early childhood education settings (e.g., facilitating peer-to-peer support, embedding IEP goal instruction into natural routines).
☐	16. *co-teach* with early childhood educators, health specialists, and others to facilitate student access to the content being taught.
☐	17. work with others to *train, direct, and supervise paraeducators* to provide learning support to students with disabilities and other students who struggle in learning.
☐	18. use *evidence-based practices* such as natural peer supports, cooperative and partner learning structures, and differentiated instruction to support meaningful inclusive experiences.
☐	19. facilitate *positive relationships among all students* (e.g., provide social interaction instruction, conduct class meetings, teach cooperative group lessons that focus upon social as well as academic skills, facilitate Circle of Friends) to promote genuine social inclusion.
☐	20. *regularly monitor* and report progress of goal attainment for students with IEPs and others who receive their services.
☐	21. work collaboratively with others to *keep parents regularly informed of student progress,* including the progress of students with disabilities on IEP and other general curriculum goals.
☐	22. work collaboratively with others to *plan for transitions* to facilitate students' movement to school-aged settings and services (e.g., kindergarten, school-aged special education support services).

Rating (0 – 4)	Indicator of Redefined Roles And Responsibilities of Early Childhood Care Providers and Educators, Special Educators, Related Services Personnel and Other Support/Health Specialists, and Paraeducators

TO BE COMPLETED BY PARAEDUCATORS

Directions for rating: Please rate each item using the following sentence starter: "In our inclusive early childhood education program, paraeducators (paraprofessionals, instructional assistants, non-certificated personnel) . . . "

☐ 23. *work under the direction and supervision* of early childhood education teachers, special educators, and/or other specialists.

☐ 24. have opportunities to *communicate and collaboratively plan* with and/or *receive training* and modeling from their supervisors on a regular (e.g., weekly) basis.

☐ 25. are *actively engaged in instruction or monitoring* students as students work independently, with partners, or in groups.

☐ 26. *implement specific curricular adaptations and instructional strategies* identified as needed to assist students with disabilities to progress in the general curriculum.

☐ 27. interact with students in ways that *build positive relationships* among peers in academic and social activities (e.g., facilitate natural peer supports and problem solving).

☐ 28. facilitate student *independence* and *natural peers supports* by avoiding being "velcroed" to (e.g., sitting next to and interacting only with) "assigned" students or students with identified "special" needs.

☐ 29. *support the classroom teacher(s) and any student* in the classroom (not just students with IEPs or other identified support needs, such as English learners), as needed.

☐ 30. *collect data* on student progress on academic, social-emotional, behavior, communication, language or other goals, as directed or needed.

EARLY CHILDHOOD CARE PROVIDERS AND EDUCATORS
(including volunteers)

Total Score (out of 36 maximum): ________

Mean Score (Total Score/9): ________

Range of Scores: ______ **(low) to** ______ **(high)**

SPECIAL EDUCATORS, RELATED SERVICES PERSONNEL, AND OTHER SUPPORT AND HEALTH SPECIALISTS

Total Score (out of 52 maximum): ________

Mean Score (Total Score/13): ________

Range of Scores: ______ **(low) to** ______ **(high)**

PARAEDUCATORS

Total Score (out of 32 maximum): ________

Mean Score (Total Score/8): ________

Range of Scores: ______ **(low) to** ______ **(high)**

References

Strain, P. S., & Smith, L. (2016, February 18). Preschool inclusion: What's the evidence, what gets in the way, and what do high-quality programs look like? [Webinar] In *2016 National Inclusion Webinar Series of the Early Childhood Technical Assistance Center*. Retrieved from http://ectacenter.org/~calls/2016/nationalinclusion.asp

U.S. Department of Health and Human Services & U.S. Department of Education. (2015, September 14). *Policy statement on inclusion of children with disabilities in early childhood programs*. Washington, D.C.: Authors. Retrieved from www2.ed.gov/policy/speced/guid/earlylearning/joint-statement-full-text.pdf

Early Childhood Inclusive Education Best Practice #4: *Collaborative Teaming*

4

Our understandings of effective collaborative teams are largely drawn from our experiences with inclusive classrooms and schools and the teams that support them (Villa & Thousand, 2017), as well as from our reading of the literature on cooperative group learning (Johnson and Johnson, 2009), collaboration and consultation (Hourcade & Bauwens, 2002), and cooperation (Brandt, 1987).

Key to successful inclusive education are opportunities to develop and practice effective and efficient collaborative teaming skills. In a national study of over 600 general and special education teachers and administrators, Villa, Thousand, Nevin, and Meyers (1996) found collaboration to be one of the top three predictors (along with administrative support and professional development) of positive attitudes toward inclusive education. Likewise, the National Center on Educational Restructuring and Inclusion (1996) found opportunities for personnel to collaborate (i.e., building-level planning teams, scheduled time for teachers to plan and teach together, effective collaboration with parents) critical to successful inclusion.

In early childhood education settings, a variety of collaborative teams exist based upon the team's defined function. Positive Behavior Intervention and Support (PBIS), Professional Development (PD), and Professional Learning Community (PLC) teams are common educational teams. Individual Education Program (IEP) planning teams exist for students eligible for special education. The overarching responsibility of any school team is to engage solution-finding strategies to solve identified problems, support instructional personnel to effectively teach and differentiate instruction, plan and implement educational and related support services that positively impact one or more students, and prevent unnecessary referral for assessment for special education eligibility.

Elements of an Effective Collaborative Teaming Process

There are five key elements to successful cooperative processes: positive interdependence, interpersonal skills, group processing, individual accountability, and frequent face-to-face interactions.

Positive Interdependence

Positive interdependence is at the heart of collaborative teaming and involves the recognition that no single person can meet the diverse psychological and educational needs of all students. Team members create the feeling of positive interdependence when they agree to share and distribute responsibility for the learning of all students for whom they are problem solving by pooling their diverse knowledge, skills, and material resources. To establish positive interdependence, team members can and should establish common goals, create celebrations jointly recognizing their effort and successes, and divide the labor for planning, implementing, and assessing the effectiveness of their plans and solutions. Distributing and rotating leadership functions (e.g., timekeeper, recorder, summarizer, encourager, agreement checker, jargon buster) also helps create a sense of positive interdependence.

Interpersonal Skills

One of the five critical elements of effective collaborative teaming is conscious attention to practicing and improving team members' interpersonal skills and relationships. Needed interpersonal skills are many and include skills in trust building, communication, conflict management, and creative problem solving. Team members often find that they are functioning at different interpersonal skill levels, depending on their previous training, mastery of curriculum content, personality styles, communication preferences, and the number of people with whom they collaborate.

Most people develop proficiency in teaming by actually working with and getting to know their teammates. An initial step, then, is to devote some meeting time to learning about teammates' cultural, personal, and professional backgrounds, as well as each member's experiences with collaborative teaming. Tapping into each other's unique cultural heritages also helps members learn about teammates' strengths and interests.

Group Processing

Group processing refers to the process of frequently debriefing about the team's successes and challenges. Team members agree to and structure into meetings time to check in with one another to determine whether the students for whom they are problem solving are making hoped for progress and teammates are maintaining and developing their interpersonal relations. Methods for self-monitoring and processing vary from simple to complex. For example, some teams use a checklist on which they each literally check off their agreed-on roles and responsibilities. Team members also can take turns sharing accomplishments, reporting on what one another contributed to the success of a student intervention, and making suggestions about what might need to be changed to improve a planned support for one or more students.

Individual Accountability

Individual accountability is the engine of collaboration. Individual accountability is a form of acknowledging the importance of the actions from each member of the collaborative team. Individual accountability involves taking time to assess the individual performance of each member of the team for one or more of four purposes. One purpose is to increase team members' perceptions of their contributions to their problem-solving endeavors. A second purpose is to provide members with recognition for their contributions. Yet another is to determine whether any adjustments need to be made in any member's roles or the team's student support actions. A final purpose is to identify when one or more of the partners may need assistance (e.g., coaching, access to additional resources or supports) to increase effectiveness in performing assigned roles and responsibilities.

Face-to-Face Interaction

Frequent and predictable face-to-face interaction is important to continuity in decision making, monitoring of implementation of team decisions, and timely adjustment of action plans. Collaborative teams are most efficient when they agree to when and how often they will meet, as well as how much time meetings will take. They need to decide when others (e.g., parents, specialists, personnel of other programs the child attends) should be involved. They also need to develop a system for communicating information when formal meetings are not scheduled.

Team membership. The most effective problem-solving teams are ones comprised of individuals with diverse backgrounds, roles, and expertise that bring together divergent skills and perspectives. We have found that an optimally effective team includes among its members, those who:

- have the needed expertise to solve the challenge (e.g., assistive technology specialist, Positive Behavior Intervention and Support (PBIS) specialist, English language development teacher/specialist);
- have direct experience with the child for whom the meeting has been convened (e.g., parents, the classroom teacher, last year's teacher, previous early childhood education program staff, paraeducator, staff of child care and recreation programs that the child attends);

- are or may be affected by the decision (e.g., after-school child care providers, a paraeducator who works with the child and who will help implement the solutions); and
- have an interest in and are invited by the person about whom the meeting has been convened (e.g., family friend, neighbor, sibling, grandparent).

Using a structured meeting agenda to increase team efficiency. Meetings are more likely to be both effective and efficient when members consistently use a structured agenda to guide their conversations. The meeting format in Figure 4.1 ensures that teams attend to the five elements of the cooperative process—positive interdependence, interpersonal skills, group processing, individual accountability, and frequent face-to-face interactions—when they meet (Villa & Thousand, 2017).

- *Positive interdependence.* Roles are rotated and assigned in advance of the next meeting so members have the materials needed to carry out their roles (e.g., the timekeeper has a watch or timer, the recorder has a computer or chart paper and markers to record minutes). Rotating roles creates a sense of distributed responsibility.
- *Interpersonal skills.* Pauses are built in for group processing at the halfway point and at the end of the meeting.
- *Individual accountability.* Members are assigned tasks with corresponding due dates.
- *Face-to-face interaction.* Members are recorded as being present, late, or absent from the meeting.

Figure 4.1 Collaborative Planning Meeting Agenda Format

People present:	Absentees:	Others who need to know:
Roles	This meeting	Next meeting
Timekeeper:		
Recorder:		
Other:		
Other:		
Agenda		
Agenda Items		*Time limit*
1. Review agenda & positive comments		5 minutes
2.		
3.		
4. Pause for group processing of progress toward task accomplishment and use of interpersonal skills		2 minutes
5.		
6.		
7. Final group processing of task and relationship		5 minutes
Minutes of Outcomes		
Action Items	*Person(s) Responsible*	*By When?*
Communicate outcomes to absent members and others by:		
1.		
2.		
3.		
Agenda Building for Next Meeting		
Date:	Time:	Location:
Expected Agenda Items		
1.		
2.		
3.		

"Are We Really a Collaborative Team?" Self-Assessment

Members of effective collaborative teams periodically check their team's "health" and plan for improvements by using tools such as the "Are We Really a Collaborative Team?" checklist shown in Figure 4.2 below. We suggest that each team member first individually rate the checklist items before the group completes the checklist as a whole. The team only checks "Yes" for an item if all members unanimously vote that way individually. This approach encourages team members to have a real dialogue about differing perceptions about the team planning experience. Have fun using this checklist to celebrate your team's growth and remind one another of what makes an effective team truly productive and enjoyable.

Figure 4.2 "Are We Really a Collaborative Team?" Self-Assessment

Directions: Check Yes or No to each of the following statements to determine your Collaboration Score at this point in time.		
Yes	**No**	**In our team planning and problem-solving team:**
Positive Interdependence		
		1. Have we publicly discussed the group's overall purpose and goals?
		2. Do we distribute leadership responsibility by rotating roles (e.g., recorder, timekeeper, encourager, agreement checker, jargon buster)?
		3. Do we start each meeting with positive comments and devote time at each meeting to celebrating successes?
		4. Do we have fun at our meetings?
Group Interpersonal Skills and Individual Accountability		
		5. Have we established norms for behavior during meetings (e.g., all members participate, active listening when others speak, no scapegoating)?
		6. Do we explain the norms to new members?
		7. Do we create a safe atmosphere for expressing genuine and potentially contradicting perspectives, and do we acknowledge conflict during meetings?

(continued on next page . . .)

Figure 4.2 (continued)

Directions: Check Yes or No to each of the following statements to determine your Collaboration Score at this point in time.		
Yes	**No**	**In our team planning and problem-solving team:**
		8. Do we have a communication system for absent members and people who need to know about our decisions, but who are not regular team members (e.g., building or district administrators)?
		9. Do we consciously identify our decision-making process (e.g., consensus, unanimous decision) for making a particular decision?
Group Processing		
		10. Do we consciously attempt to improve our interpersonal skills (e.g., perspective taking, creative problem solving, conflict resolution) by setting time aside to reflect upon and discuss our interactions and feelings?
		11. Do we consciously attempt to improve our interpersonal skills by setting interpersonal goals for our next meeting time?
Face-to-Face Interaction		
		12. Do we have regularly scheduled meetings that are held at times and locations agreed upon in advance by teammates?
		13. When we meet, do we arrange ourselves so we can see and hear each other (i.e., in a circle)?
		14. Do we use a structured agenda format that prescribes and identifies agenda items for the meeting and sets time limits for each agenda item?
		15. Are needed members invited? Do they receive a timely invitation? (Note: Needed members change from meeting to meeting based upon agenda items.)
		16. Do we start and end on time?
		TOTAL

Early Childhood Inclusive Education Best Practice Checklist Assessment

Best Practice #4: *Collaborative Teaming*

Directions: Based upon your experience, please give each of the 13 indicators a (zero to 4) rating in response to the question, "To what degree does this best practice occur in our early childhood education setting(s)?"

4	3	2	1	0
Always	Most of the time	Some of the time	Rarely	Never

Rating (0 – 4) **Indicator of Collaborative Teaming**

☐ 1. Team members *regularly collaborate* with one another to plan, instruct, and evaluate the performance of students with and without disabilities.

☐ 2. For teams focused upon individual students, team members *regularly communicate and share information* about student strengths, needs, and services outside of team meetings.

☐ 3. Among an early childhood program's teams is a *creative problem-solving team* (e.g., MTSS or PBIS team described in Chapters 8 and 9), which *meets regularly* to *assist early childhood educators to address individual student challenges* (e.g., academic, social-emotional/interpersonal, communication) and avoid unnecessary referrals for special education eligibility.

☐ 4. The *assistance* provided by the program's creative problem-solving team is of high quality and *results in useful and usable solutions* and interventions to identified problems.

☐ 5. The *membership* of school problem-solving teams includes *individuals with the needed expertise* (e.g.,

Rating (0 – 4)	Indicator of Collaborative Teaming
	assistive technology specialist, Positive Behavior Intervention and Support (PBIS) specialist, English language development teacher/specialist) to solve the problem.
☐	6. The *membership* of school problem-solving teams includes individuals with *direct experience* (e.g., parents, the classroom teacher, last year's teacher, previous early childhood education program staff, paraeducator, staff of child care and recreation programs that the child attends) with the student for whom the meeting has been convened.
☐	7. The membership of school problem-solving teams includes the *individual(s) affected by the decision* (e.g., after-school child care providers, a paraeducator who works with the child and who will help implement the solutions).
☐	8. The *membership* of school problem-solving teams includes *individuals who have an interest in the child* (e.g., family friend, neighbor, sibling, grandparent) for whom the meeting is being held.
☐	9. Adequate *planning time* is provided for early childhood program personnel and other team members to collaborate.
☐	10. Teams use a *structured agenda format:* such as that presented in Figure 4.1: to be efficient and effective and to promote positive interdependence, interpersonal skills, group processing, individual accountability, and face-to-face interaction.
☐	11. Members of early childhood education collaborative teams *periodically check* their team's *"health," celebrate* their growth, and *plan for improvements* by using a tool such as the "Are We Really a Collaborative Team?" checklist shown in Figure 4.2.

Rating (0 – 4)	Indicator of Collaborative Teaming
☐	12. Team members know and use a variety of *creative problem-solving strategies* (e.g., brainstorming, seeking additional information through questioning, meta-cognition, asking for the underlying rationale for a proposed solution, asking for critical feedback) to address issues.
☐	13. Team members have received *training in collaborative teaming and creative problem-solving processes.*

Total Score (out of 52 maximum): ________

Mean Score (Total Score/13): ________

Range of Scores: ______ **(low) to** ______ **(high)**

References

Brandt, R. (1987). On cooperation in schools: A conversation with David and Roger Johnson. *Educational Leadership, 44*(3), 14-19.

Hourcade, J., & Bauwens, J. (2002). *Cooperative teaching: Rebuilding and sharing the schoolhouse.* Austin, TX: Pro-Ed.

Johnson, D. W., & Johnson, F. P. (2005). *Joining together: Group theory and skills* (9th ed.). Needham Heights, MA: Allyn & Bacon.

National Center on School Restructuring and Inclusion. (1996). *National study on inclusive education.* New York, NY: City University of New York.

Villa, R. A., & Thousand, J. S. (2017). *Leading an inclusive school: Access and success for all.* Alexandria, VA: Association for Supervision and Curriculum Development.

Villa, R., Thousand, J., Nevin, A., & Meyers, H. (1996). Teacher and administrator perceptions of heterogeneous education. *Exceptional Children, 65,* 29-45.

Early Childhood Inclusive Education Best Practice #5: *Co-Teaching*

5

Co-teaching may be defined as two or more people sharing responsibility for teaching all of the students assigned to a classroom (Villa, Thousand, & Nevin, 2013). Features of effective co-teaching include the distribution of responsibility among the co-teachers for planning, instructing, and evaluating the performance of their assigned students in mixed-ability classrooms. A common co-teaching partnership is that between an early childhood educator (a master of content) and a special educator (a master of access). Although this is the prevalent configuration, anyone can co-teach. Co-teaching teams may include Head Start teachers, public and private child care providers, related service personnel such as speech and language pathologists, English language learning specialists, therapists, other support and health specialists, paraeducators, volunteers, and other community partners (Nevin, Villa, & Thousand, 2009).

Co-teaching has been found to be effective in supporting students with a variety of needs. Emerging research suggests that co-teaching allows for differentiation of instruction and curriculum access for all students. Namely, co-teaching increases the teacher-student ratio, provides students with access to the diverse and specialized knowledge and instructional approaches of their co-teachers, and enables co-teachers to more readily use evidence-based teaching strategies (e.g., cooperative group learning). Co-teaching has been found to increase overall student achievement, decrease referrals for behavior interventions or more intensive services, and result in happier teachers who feel less isolated (Schwab Learning, 2003; Villa et al., 2013). Further, students with and without disabilities report having positive experiences in co-taught classrooms (Wilson & Michaels, 2006).

In successful co-teaching partnerships, where co-teachers move in and out of four co-teaching approaches based upon student needs and curriculum demands, students view their co-teachers as knowledgeable and credible. The four co-teaching approaches—supportive, parallel, complementary, and team—are defined and described in Table 1 (Villa et al., 2013). Recent research has been conducted to assess the impact of the application of the four co-teaching approaches on evidence-based practices in early childhood settings. Namely, observations of co-teaching partners in 74 co-taught preschool (pre-kindergarten through kindergarten) classrooms in Kansas revealed that when co-teachers went beyond simply using the supportive co-teaching approach and also employed one or more of the other three co-teaching approaches, student engagement and performance increased (Anderson, 2018; Gaumer Erickson, 2019). Specifically, when co-teachers applied multiple co-teaching approaches, they were more likely to explicitly teach behavioral and academic procedures, check for understanding, provide prompts and cues, reinforce effort and social/behavioral expectations, and provide specific feedback. Additionally, students were more likely to follow academic and behavioral procedures and be engaged with peers in their work and responding when multiple approaches were used.

Figure 5.1 The Four Co-Teaching Approaches Defined

Supportive co-teaching is when one teacher takes the lead instructional role while the other teacher(s) rotate(s) among students and provide(s) support. For example, the supportive co-teacher watches and listens as students work, stepping in to provide assistance as needed, while the lead teacher continues to direct the overall lesson.

Parallel co-teaching is when two or more people work with different groups of students in different sections of the classroom. Station teaching at centers and monitoring of students working with peers in cooperative groupings are examples of this approach.

Complementary co-teaching is when a co-teacher enhances the instruction provided by the other co-teacher. For example, one co-teacher might paraphrase the other's statements, draw or provide visuals, model a procedure being described by the other co-teacher, or provide additional examples.

Team co-teaching is when two or more people do what the traditional teacher has done alone—plan, teach, assess, and assume responsibility for all of the students in the classroom. They both deliver content and both employ strategies to facilitate access to the curriculum. This approach has the most equitable distribution of duties. For example, co-teachers might jointly role-play a social skill (e.g., taking turns, using quiet voices, sharing materials).

Early Childhood Inclusive Education Best Practice Checklist Assessment

Best Practice #5: *Co-Teaching*

Directions: Based upon your experience, please give each of the 15 indicators a (zero to 4) rating in response to the question, "To what degree does this best practice occur in our early childhood education setting(s)?"

4	3	2	1	0
Always	**Most of the time**	**Some of the time**	**Rarely**	**Never**

Rating (0 – 4) **Indicator of Co-Teaching**

☐ 1. There is *widespread use of co-teaching* (i.e., two or more people sharing instructional responsibility for all of the students assigned to them) at the program site.

☐ 2. Co-teachers *share responsibility* for planning, teaching, and assessing the progress of all the students they share in common.

☐ 3. Regardless of which co-teaching approach is used, *all co-teachers* work with *all students* assigned to a classroom.

☐ 4. Co-teaching is viewed as a vehicle to provide quality *differentiated instruction.*

☐ 5. Co-teaching is *not viewed as voluntary,* but as required to ensure student support and curriculum access.

☐ 6. In addition to virtual planning (e.g., sharing of materials via e-mail or Google docs) partners who co-teach (e.g., early childhood educators, special educators, English language development teachers, related service providers, paraeducators) meet and collaboratively *plan face-to-face at least weekly* for a minimum of 45-60 minutes a week.

Rating (0 – 4)	Indicator of Co-Teaching
☐	7. On average, *co-taught early childhood classrooms* have *no more than 1/3 or 33%* of the students in a class identified as *eligible for special education services,* unless it is reflective of the demographic of the total school district population.
☐	8. Co-taught classrooms are *comprised of a mix of students who represent the overall population of the school district* (e.g., academic and social performance, primary language, ethnic and cultural background, race, gender) rather than primarily students who struggle to learn or are considered at risk or lower achieving.
☐	9. Co-teaching partners or teams *regularly remain together* for more than one year.
☐	10. When using *parallel* co-teaching (i.e., students taught in groups) the *vast majority* of the time, students work in *heterogeneous, mixed-ability groups.*
☐	11. In *parallel* co-teaching, when students are *grouped homogeneously,* groupings are *fluid and flexible* and based upon *analysis of student performance data* rather than eligibility for special education or other services.
☐	12. In *parallel* co-teaching, when students are grouped homogeneously, students are *not grouped based upon a particular label* (e.g., eligible for special education, English learner), but based upon the need for extension or a particular instructional intervention or strategy.
☐	13. Co-teachers use *all four* co-teaching approaches (i.e., supportive, parallel, complementary, team) rather than relying primarily on supportive and/or parallel approaches.

Rating (0 – 4)	Indicator of Collaborative Teaming
☐	14. Co-teaching approaches are *regularly used at all three tiers* (i.e., core, supplemental, and intensive) of the program's Multi-Tiered System of Supports (MTSS). (See Chapter 8 for details regarding MTSS.)
☐	15. Co-teaching approaches are *regularly used at all three tiers* (i.e., core, supplemental, and intensive) of the program's Positive Behavior Interventions and Supports (PBIS) system. (See Chapter 9 for details regarding PBIS systems.)

Total Score (out of 60 maximum): ________

Mean Score (Total Score/15): ________

Range of Scores: ______ **(low) to** _______ **(high)**

References

Anderson, S. (2018, November 16). Teach together: Co-teaching in early childhood settings. In the *Early Learning Webinar Series of Kansas State Department of Education, Division of Learning Services.* Retrieved from https://ksde-tasn-webinar.adobeconnect.com/pzmvh1ruqa8h

Gaumer Erickson, A. S. (2019). *Early childhood co-taught classroom observations: Preliminary analysis.* Unpublished manuscript, Center for Research on Learning, University of Kansas, Lawrence, KS.

Nevin, A. I., Villa, R. A., & Thousand, J. S. (2009). *A guide to co-teaching with paraeducators: Practical tips for K-12 educators.* Thousand Oaks, CA: Corwin Press.

Schwab Learning (2003). Collaboratively speaking: A study on effective ways to teach children with learning differences in the general education classroom. *The Special EDge, 16*(3), 1-4.

Villa, R. A., Thousand, J. S., & Nevin, A. I. (2013). *A guide to co-teaching: New lessons and strategies to facilitate student learning* (3rd ed.). Thousand Oaks, CA: Corwin Press.

Wilson, G. L., & Michaels, C.A. (2006). General and special education students' perceptions of co-teaching: Implications for secondary-level literacy instruction. *Reading & Writing Quarterly: Overcoming Learning Difficulties, 22*(3), 205-225.

Early Childhood Inclusive Education Best Practice #6:

Structuring Intentional, Sufficient, and Supported Natural Peer Interactions

6

Throughout each day, children take part in a host of activities and interactions with other children and adults. All children, particularly young children, learn and develop through these interactions. Research suggests that prompting and development of peer social behavior and interaction often are neglected by early childhood care providers (Bovey & Strain, 2005). One empirically supported element of effective preschool inclusion is the "intentional, sufficient, and supported interactions between peers with and without disabilities" (Barton & Smith, 2015, p. 36).

It is noteworthy that the "positive social outcomes attributable to inclusive settings . . . have been seen only when social interaction is frequent, planned, and carefully promoted by teachers" (Strain, 2014, p. 1). Therefore, in early childhood education and care settings, it is critical that the adults who staff these programs recognize the importance of and are skilled in planning and arranging interaction opportunities likely to achieve one or more of the following desired outcomes for young children with and without disabilities: (1) superior learning in communication and cognitive development, (2) social-emotional learning and development, (3) being a valued and accepted member of peer groups (i.e., friendships), and (4) maintenance and transfer of skills across time and place.

Often, young children with disabilities need more intentionally structured and facilitated experiences in order to achieve the above outcomes. For example, it has been demonstrated that children are more likely, over time, to develop and use prosocial behaviors with peers when their teachers and care providers deliberately use prompts and cues to engage children in using desired social behaviors (Bovey & Strain, 2005). Prompting strategies include behavioral momentum and priming.

Behavioral momentum involves asking a child to do something that he or she is good at, providing lots of positive attention, and then immediately requesting the child to do something that is more difficult. For example, Josue, who has difficulty initiating interactions with peers, enjoys jumping on the trampoline. Immediately after jumping, an adult can ask Josue to invite Desiree to play with him at the water table. *Priming* involves offering children ideas on how to engage in social activities before the activity starts. An example of priming is an adult asking, "Who are you going to invite to play with you in the dress up area?" and rehearsing with a child how to ask a peer to join in. Prompting strategies should always be followed by acknowledgment and reinforcement to increase the likelihood that the desired prosocial behaviors will occur again. To ensure generalization, transfer, and maintenance of social interaction skills, these strategies should be used widely across settings and personnel.

Intentional structuring of peer interactions also involves direct instruction, modeling, and guided practice in social interactional skills, including conflict resolution, through planned activities such as puppet shows, group conversations, and scripts. For example, adults can enhance the problem-solving skills of children by teaching and practicing self-control and problem-solving scripts. Consider the POP and WIN scripts used by preschool and early primary school educators (Villa, Thousand, & Nevin, 2010).

POP

- **Problem?**
- **Options?**
- **Plan?**

WIN

- **What is the problem?**
- **Identify possible solutions.**
- **Narrow it down to the best choice.**

While early childhood educational experiences offer important foundations for future academic success, the social interactional experiences that occur and are structured in this early period of child development have been found to be far more important than early academics in predicting not only future success in school, but well-being in adulthood. Namely, while controlling for family demographics and early academic ability, Jones, Green, and Crowley's (2015) nearly 20-year longitudinal study found statistically significant correlations between measured social-emotional skills in kindergarten and multiple measures of adult well-being (i.e., education, employment, criminal activity, substance use, mental health) at age 25. These findings emphasize the critical importance of early childhood educators and care providers structuring intentional, sufficient, and supported natural peer interactions.

Additional ways in which to structure and support natural peer interactions and social-emotional learning are included in the following best practice indicators.

Early Childhood Inclusive Education Best Practice Checklist Assessment

Best Practice #6:
Structuring Intentional, Sufficient, and Supported Natural Peer Interactions

Directions: Based upon your experience, please give each of the 14 indicators a (zero to 4) rating in response to the question, "To what degree does this best practice occur in our early childhood education setting(s)?"

4	3	2	1	0
Always	**Most of the time**	**Some of the time**	**Rarely**	**Never**

Rating (0 – 4)	Indicator of Structuring Intentional, Sufficient, and Supported Natural Peer Interactions
☐	1. Early childhood educators and care providers *intentionally organize* materials and physical space to *facilitate natural peer interactions.*
☐	2. Early childhood educators and care providers *intentionally promote* a sense of *membership* and *belonging* by focusing upon children's strengths and modeling positive verbal and nonverbal behavior and responses (Soukakou, 2016).
☐	3. Early childhood educators and care providers embed activities that *promote understanding of diversity and individual differences* through the use of visuals, characters in stories, role play, puppets, and so forth (Soukakou, 2016).
☐	4. Early childhood educators and care providers *teach and practice* predictable *procedures, routines, and signals.*
☐	5. When intervening to help children resolve conflict, early childhood educators and care providers *focus upon what children could do* (i.e., guide children to discover alternative prosocial ways of interacting with peers) *rather than focusing upon what children should not do.*

Rating (0 - 4)	Indicator of Structuring Intentional, Sufficient, and Supported Natural Peer Interactions
☐	6. Early childhood educators and care providers structure play and other experiences so that *children with varying levels or degrees of social developmental competence are grouped together.*
☐	7. When needed, early childhood educators and care providers *employ multiple means of communication,* including augmentative and assistive technology (e.g., sign language, iPads, the PECS Picture Exchange Communication System), to *facilitate communication* among and participation with peers.
☐	8. Early childhood educators and care providers *use prompting strategies* such as the behavioral momentum and priming strategies described in the previous text.
☐	9. For older children who appear to lack confidence, early childhood educators and care providers provide *opportunities for them to be paired with socially skilled younger children* (Kemple, 1992).
☐	10. For a child having difficulty entering ongoing play, early childhood educators and care providers (a) *guide the child to a smaller group or a group with members who are likely to be more accepting,* or (b) *translate* for the group members the desire or *intentions of the child attempting to join.* (E.g., If Amaya wants to join a group and wants the role of big sister, an adult could say, "Amaya wanted to be the big sister. That role is taken by Arden. Who else could Amaya be?")
☐	11. Early childhood educators and care providers *provide direct instruction, modeling, and guided practice* in social skills, including conflict resolution, through planned activities such as puppet shows, group conversations, and scripts. For example, early childhood educators and care providers teach and practice self-control and problem-solving scripts such as the POP and WIN scripts described in the previous text.

Rating (0 – 4)	Indicator of Structuring Intentional, Sufficient, and Supported Natural Peer Interactions
☐	12. Early childhood educators and care providers *develop and use scripted social stories* (Grey, 2015) to help a child understand, predict, and successfully engage in social interactions, situations, routines, expectations or rules, cues, and unfamiliar activities.
☐	13. Early childhood educators and care providers provide *on-the-spot guidance to facilitate communication* and successful play and other interactions. For example, for a child having difficulty reading the emotional and facial cues of another child, an adult might say, "Jacque, look at Rich's face. Do you think he likes it when you pinch him?"
☐	14. When conflicts arise, early childhood educators and care providers provide *on-the-spot guidance in conflict resolution* by encouraging the involved children to identify their thoughts and feelings, generate potential solutions, and come to a mutually agreeable solution. When possible, they use a problem-solving script the children already know, such as the POP and WIN scripts described in the previous text.

Total Score (out of 56 maximum): ________

Mean Score (Total Score/14): ________

Range of Scores: ______ **(low) to** _______ **(high)**

References

Barton, E. E., & Smith, B. J. (2015). *The preschool inclusion toolbox: How to build and lead a high-quality program.* Baltimore, MD: Paul H. Brookes Publishing Co., Inc.

Bovey, T. & Strain, P. (2005). *Strategies for increasing peer social interactions: Prompting and acknowledgment.* Nashville, TN: Center on the Social and Emotional Foundations for Early Learning, Vanderbilt Peabody College of Education and Human Development, Vanderbilt University. Retrieved from http://csefel.uiuc.edu/breifs/wwb17.pdf

Grey, C. (2015). *The new social story book, revised and expanded 15th anniversary edition.* Arlington, TX: Future Horizons.

Jones, D. E., Green, M., & Crowley, M. (2015). Early social-emotional functioning and public health: The relationship between kindergarten social competence and future wellness. *American Journal of Public Health, 105*(11), 2285-2290.

Kemple, K. M. (1992). *Understanding and facilitating preschool children's peer acceptance.* Retrieved from ERIC Clearinghouse on Elementary and Early Childhood Education database, www.ericdigests.org/1992-3/preschool.htm. (ED345866)

Strain, P. (2014). *Inclusion for preschool children with disabilities: What we know and what we should be doing.* Retrieved from https://ectacenter.org/~pdfs/topics/inclusion/research/STRAIN_what_we_know.pdf

Soukakou, E. P. (2016). *Inclusive classroom profile (ICPTM): Research edition.* Baltimore, MD: Paul H. Brookes Publishing Co., Inc.

Villa, R. A., Thousand, J. S., & Nevin, A. I. (2010). *Collaborating with students in instruction and decision making: The untapped resource.* Thousand Oaks, CA: Corwin Press.

7 Early Childhood Inclusive Education Best Practice #7:

Student-Centered, Strength-Based Assessment and Differentiated Instruction

As we learned in Chapter 1, inclusive education is both the vision and practice of welcoming, valuing, empowering, and supporting the diverse academic, social-emotional, language, and communication learning of all children in shared environments and experiences for the purpose of attaining the desired goals of education. Inclusive education is a *belief* that everyone belongs and that all are valued and contributing members of the community. Inclusive education also is the *practice* of differentiating instruction for children through collaborative planning and teaching among all members of a school and learning community, including students and families.

What is Differentiated Instruction?

Differentiated instruction is a way for educators and early childhood care providers to recognize and react responsively to the varying background knowledge, readiness, language, culture, preferences in learning, and interests of the children they serve (Thousand, Villa, & Nevin, 2015). It is a way to plan for and respond to individual differences via a process of adapting and modifying materials, learning goals, instructional methods and learning activities, and what children are expected to do and produce in a classroom (Universal Design for Learning, 2013). Stated otherwise, differentiated instruction requires providing children with multiple means of *representation* (content differentiation), multiple means of *engagement* (process differentiation), and multiple means of *action* and *expression* (product differentiation). Differentiation requires attention to the following four access design points when planning activities and instruction:

1. Facts about the learners—children's learning strengths, preferences and challenges, levels of readiness and interest, and best ways of communicating
2. Content and materials—what children are expected to learn, know, and do, and the materials they interact with to access that content
3. Processes of learning—how learning activities are structured to facilitate students making sense of what they are learning
4. Products and assessments—how children demonstrate and how early childhood educators and care providers assess what is learned

Student-Centered, Strength-Based Assessment

The process of differentiating instruction begins with early childhood educators and care providers getting to know their learners by gathering facts (data) about and developing profiles of the abilities, strengths, and learning challenges of children. Learner data can and should be gathered in a variety of ways (Division for Early Childhood, 2014), including direct observations of children in everyday situations, ethnographic interviews (Westby, 1990), and surveys of primary caregivers. Data also may be gathered through dynamic transdisciplinary play-based assessment approaches, which have proven not only to be authentic, family-centered, cost-efficient ways of getting to know a child and his/her family (Gutierrez-Clellen & Peña, 2001; Myers, McBride, & Peterson, 1996), but also a vehicle for cross-disciplinary professional learning of all involved (King et al., 2009).

Two person- and family-centered processes that are particularly appealing for gathering information about a young child are Making Action Plans or MAPs (Falvey, Forest, Pearpoint, & Rosenberg, 2002; Thousand et al., 2015) and Pathways: A Child and Family Journey© (Moore, Hyde-Smith, Pratt, & McKnight, 2011). Both processes engage a group of people who have various relationships with a child—parents, siblings, neighbors, friends, teachers, early childhood care providers, and anyone else the family chooses to invite—to highlight what they know about the child's strengths, likes and dislikes, and his/her learning, social-emotional, and communication characteristics in order to creatively plan for a child's future in the context of his/her family, culture, and community. Table 7.1 identifies and describes the seven key questions that a facilitator of a MAPs meeting asks and memorializes in writing. Pathways directions and a graphic organizer that families can use to memorialize answers to a set of suggested questions in advance of face-to-face meetings with professionals may be found at www.balswan.org/s/2014-15PathwaysForm.pdf.

Differentiating Instruction Using a Universal Design for Learning Approach

The Universal Design for Learning (UDL) approach to differentiated instruction involves designing environments, materials, experiences, and assessments, so that adaptations for particular circumstances or children are not needed or are less likely to be needed. UDL is always a proactive approach. With the UDL differentiation approach, early childhood educators and care providers presume diversity and *first* gather facts about *all* of their learners along multiple dimensions of their diversity (e.g., strengths, developmental interests and preferences, cultural background, means of communication). They get to know children by observing their participation in everyday routines and activities that comprise their learning opportunities and experiences.

With this information in mind, early childhood educators and care providers now think about and plan for how they will provide multiple representations of the material to be experienced or learned, multiple means of engagement to help children make sense of what they are to do and learn, and multiple means for children to express progress and show what they have learned. To differentiate at the content access design point, educators and care providers determine and use materials (e.g., building supplies, play structures, toys) and adult interactional and instructional behaviors that are most likely to prompt optimal levels of each child's competence. To differentiate at the process access design point, educators and care providers use strengths-based everyday activities and context-specific instructional and interactional practices to facilitate children's engagement, learning, and expression of interests and skills. To differentiate at the product access design point, educators and care providers use informal (e.g., observation) and formal (e.g., direct, curriculum-based) assessment approaches to monitor and analyze children's learning and progress in order to adjust learning opportunities, as needed.

Differentiating Instruction Using the Mismatch and Solution-Finding Differentiation Process

The Mismatch and Solution-Finding Differentiation Process is a systematic process an educational team can use to identify and resolve mismatches between the instruction that typically has been provided in a classroom and the attributes of children with more diverse learning, communication, behavioral, or other characteristics than team members have been accustomed. When the process is used ahead of engaging in an activity or lesson in order to redesign the content, process, and product demands of the experience, it is a *proactive* differentiation process. When the process is used after the fact—when it is discovered that there are mismatches between one or more child's attributes and what originally had been planned or typically had been done—it is a *reactive* differentiation process.

Whether used proactively or reactively, the Mismatch and Solution-Finding Differentiation Process can be activated to alter the content, processes, and product demands of any experience in order to resolve the mismatch. The Mismatch and

Solution-Finding Differentiation Process Template, shown in Figure 7.1 and applied to Danika, a four-year-old with an IEP, and the activities of her inclusive early childhood classroom, illustrates how data about children and classroom demands can be compared to identify and address potential mismatches. The process illustrated in Figure 7.1 works as follows:

- The left column prompts gathering positive information as well as specific goals and needs regarding a child of concern.
- The second column prompts examination of the typical demands of an activity, lesson, or class, with particular attention to the content and materials used, products generated, along with assessment practices and the typical instructional processes employed.
- The third column prompts a comparison of the information in the first two columns in order to identify mismatches between how the child best accesses information and how content is typically delivered; between how a child best shows what s/he knows and how growth is typically assessed; or between how the child makes sense of learning and how instruction typically has been delivered.
- The fourth column is used to generate and record multiple (e.g., at least three to five) potential solutions for addressing each mismatch, with strengths, preferences, and interests of a child in mind. A team may select or combine solutions that seem most promising. The more challenges a child is perceived as presenting, the more important it is to use that child's strengths to identify mismatch solutions.

Table 7.2 lists the potential solutions Danika's team generated for each of the six mismatches identified in the third column of Table 7.1. To complete a plan of action for Danika, her team now needs to generate and apply selection criteria (e.g., uses Danika's strengths and communication systems, is least intrusive, uses natural peer supports, increases scaffolding for other students who may need prompting) in order to decide which solutions to implement. Teams are advised to memorialize in writing agreed-upon solutions so that the procedures for carrying out and collecting data on the success of each solution are clearly articulated and understood by team members. By clearly articulating solutions, teams can hold one another accountable for implementing component parts of each solution for which they are responsible and measuring progress in a timely fashion.

Table 7.1 The Key MAPs Questions for Families of Young Children

1. What is MAPs?

MAPs is an interactive process designed to assist a child and his/her family to get from where they are to where they want to be (goals).

2. What is the child's and family's history or story?

The family and, when appropriate, the child, are asked to describe the child's history or story.

3. What is the dream?

This is in many ways the most important step of the process because it identifies the dreams or goals for which you will develop a plan of action. Again, the family members, including the child, speak first and then others in attendance may add to the list of dreams. The facilitator must be nonjudgmental in both words and body language.

4. What is the nightmare?

This question helps those in attendance to understand the fears and concerns of the family for their child—the things they want to avoid. At times, this step elicits emotions and reactions that are strong and/or sad. The information is critical because the entire point of the process is to achieve the dream while avoiding the nightmare.

5. Who is the child? What are the child's strengths and gifts?

At this step, participants brainstorm and generate a list of words that describe the child for whom the MAPs is being held. The facilitator oftentimes groups descriptors into themes (e.g., learning, friendship, health). Particular emphasis is placed upon the learner's "giftedness."

6. What does the child and family need?

Participants consider what resources and supports will be needed to assist the child to reach the dream and avoid the nightmare. Those assembled may need to consider academic, communication, social-emotional, movement, health, safety, and security needs of the child.

7. What is the plan of action?

The final step is the development of a plan that includes the who, the what, and the when of actualizing the dreams and avoiding the nightmares.

Figure 7.1 Mismatch and Solution-Finding Differentiation Process Template Applied to Danika and the Demands of her Classroom Activities

Facts about the Learner **Name:** Danika	**Facts About the Environment/Activities**	**Mismatch Between Student Facts and Activity Facts**	**Potential Solutions to Mismatches Between Facts**
Characteristics and Strengths • Kinesthetic learner • Active—moves frequently from one activity to another • Enjoys & good at trampoline • Learns well with hands-on materials & activities • Musical—moves and dances to music • Assertive about her wants—takes materials she wants from others • Vocalizes loudly when excited or upset • Protests and refuses when expected to clean up or put materials away • Sometimes takes her clothes off and runs around the classroom • Happy working alone	**Materials and Activities** Teacher-led large group activities Free choice/play stations: • Dress up clothes • Drawing • Theatre with hand puppets • Sand table with toys and vehicles • Water table with floatables • Legos • Kitchen Teacher-directed and guided stations • Literacy • Math/science • Arts Minimal use of visual cues, sign language, or other signals	• During large group activities children are expected to sit and attend; Danika is active, kinesthetic & has difficulty sitting for more than a few minutes • Sharing materials with others is an expectation & goal; Danika currently does not share her materials with classmates & grabs objects she wants to play with from others • Children expected to initiate play & conversation with peers with limited prompting; Danika has limited communication (i.e., sign & pictures) to initiate	

(continued on next page . . .)

Figure 7.1 (continued)

Facts about the Learner **Name:** Danika	**Facts About the Environment/Activities**	**Mismatch Between Student Facts and Activity Facts**	**Potential Solutions to Mismatches Between Facts**
IEP Goals • Share materials • Take turns in group activities • Transition from one activity & environment to another using a picture schedule • Put away materials • Recognize her printed first name • Recognize and differentiate shapes—circle, square, triangle • Use sign language or picture communication system to: - Use functional daily living words - Initiate interactions with peers - Request a partner for play or work - Answer yes/no questions - Answer "what" questions - Indicate need to use the bathroom	**Social and Verbal Expectations** • Students expected to initiate play & conversation with peers with minimal prompting • Students expected to answer teacher questions & follow verbal directions with minimal prompting **Transitions** • Teacher(s) signal transitions & clean up with only verbal directions • Students expected to transition with minimal verbal prompting	• Danika has goals to communicate with sign & picture communication system; to date systems are being used minimally • Students are expected to clean up & transition with minimal prompting; Danika protests & refuses to clean up & put materials away • Danika sometimes takes her clothes off & runs around classroom; violates class norms	

Table 7.2 Solutions Generated by Danika's Team for Mismatches Between Danika's Characteristics and Expectations and Activities in Her Preschool Classroom

1. During large group activities, students are expected to sit and attend.
   Danika is active, kinesthetic & has difficulty sitting for more than a few minutes.
   a) Shorten expectations for how long Danika must sit
   b) Reinforce her sitting behavior
   c) Provide for movement breaks
   d) Build in whole group movement during large group activities
   e) Provide a "wiggle" stool of cushion and flexible seating
   f) Give Danika a fidget toy to play with
   g) Provide a movement activity prior to large-group activities
   h) Let Danika sit on a grown-up's lap
   i) Incorporate music with accompanying movement into the activity
   j) Provide a time that she can see, so she knows how long she has to stay

2. Sharing materials with others is an expectation & goal.
   Danika currently does not share her materials with classmates & grabs objects she wants to play with from others.
   a) Reinforce and provide incentives to everyone who shares
   b) Read stories with class about sharing behavior
   c) Create and use a social story about sharing and not sharing
   d) Role play and model sharing behavior
   e) Teach Danika how to request using visuals, including her picture communications
   f) Teach her and all of the other students signs for requesting
   g) Use songs about sharing
   h) Have available multiple objects that Danika prefers to deter grabbing objects from others
   i) Offer an incentive of extra trampoline time if she chooses another object rather than grabbing
   j) Create and use activities where children have to pass objects and take turns

3. Students are expected to initiate play & conversation with peers with limited prompting.
   Danika has limited communication (i.e., sign & pictures) to initiate.
   a) Teach Danika's signs and picture communication system to all of the students
   b) Model for Danika and classmates how to initiate play and conversation

(continued on next page . . .)

Table 7.2 (continued)

c) Reinforce Danika and classmates when they are engaged in play or conversation that Danika initiates
d) Expand the use of augmentative communication technology
e) Use video modeling of initiating play and conversation
f) Facilitate interaction with 3 or 4 select responsive peers throughout the day
g) Play games where students move to music and stop to initiate conversation about teacher-selected topics using Danika's signs, pictures, as well as words and sentence frames
h) Use puppets to pre-teach conversation prompts
i) Require Danika to use her communication system to request engagement with a preferred activity (e.g., trampoline)

4. Danika has goals to communicate with sign & picture communication system.
   To date systems are being used minimally.
   a) Train all staff in the use of Danika's sign and picture communication system
   b) Expand the use of assistive technology that she can use with an iPad
   c) When planning lessons, consciously plan how to use Danika's signs and communication system to offer Danika access to content, engage her in learning, and let her show what she knows
   d) Have speech and language pathologist co-teach to train, model, and provide feedback to adults and students supporting Danika
   e) Follow the phases of PECS
   f) Collect data on when the sign and picture communication systems are and are not being used
   g) Find out why the systems are not being used
   h) Provide staff with a "cheat sheet" to remind them of the communication steps to follow
   i) Make sure there is a PECS book with Danika at all times and in all settings
   j) Integrate the use of sign and pictures by all students several times a day

5. Students expected to follow directions to clean up & transition with minimal prompting.
   Danika protests & refuses to clean up & put materials away.
   a) Don't have her clean up – choose your battles
   b) Add songs and movement to clean-up and transitions "Pick it up; now do a jump!" The more Danika picks up, the more she gets to jump
   c) Provide hand-under-hand assistance during clean-up activities

(continued on next page . . .)

Table 7.2 (continued)

d) Provide a 2-minute, 1-minute, and 30-second warning before time to clean up
e) Use a picture schedule that includes transition and clean-up pictures
f) Use a "first-then" board
g) Break the clean-up process into smaller activities and reinforce each step of the process
h) Make Danika a teacher helper to signal clean-up time
i) Schedule time for Danika's preferred activities after clean-up
j) Use a token economy system to reinforce (with reducing prompts) transitions and clean-up

6. Danika sometimes takes her clothes off & runs around classroom, violating class norms.
   a) Determine the function of the behavior
   b) Identify and collect data on triggers, antecedents, and time of day
   c) When possible, ignore
   d) Have Danika wear clothes that are difficult to remove (e.g., romper)
   e) Ask Danika about her clothing preferences
   f) Occupy and distract her with preferred activities when she is most likely to do this
   g) Talk with the family and see if and when she does this at home
   h) Create a social story about wearing clothes
   i) See if Danika would be willing to wear a bathing suit under her clothes and agree to keep that on
   j) Consult with an occupational therapist about potential sensory issues
   k) Give Danika a doll whose clothes she can take off and put on
   l) Provide positive reinforcement throughout the day when she is wearing her clothes

Early Childhood Inclusive Education Best Practice Checklist Assessment

Best Practice #7:
Student-Centered, Strength-Based Assessment and Differentiated Instruction

Directions: Based upon your experience, please give each of the 11 indicators a (zero to 4) rating in response to the question, "To what degree does this best practice occur in our early childhood education setting(s)?"

4	3	2	1	0
Always	Most of the time	Some of the time	Rarely	Never

Rating (0 – 4)	Indicator of Student-Centered, Strength-Based Assessment and Differentiated Instruction
☐	1. Members of the IEP team of each young child *gather strength-based data* about the child and his/her family in a *variety of ways,* including direct observations in everyday situations; ethnographic interviews; surveys of primary caregivers; and dynamic, family-centered, transdisciplinary assessments (e.g., MAPs, Pathways: A Child and Family Journey©) in order to get to know the child's strengths in the context of his/her family, culture, and community.
☐	2. *Family member input* regarding their child's strengths and needs, as well as ideas for effective adaptations and accommodations, are both *solicited and considered.*
☐	3. Assessment reports and the present level of performance statements on the IEP are *written in language that describes the child's current strengths* (skills, preferences, current performance, means of communication) rather than what the child does not yet know or do.

Rating (0 – 4)	Indicator of Student-Centered, Strength-Based Assessment and Differentiated Instruction
☐	4. IEP team members *use a child's strengths, interests, and preferences,* as well as other assessment data (observations, family input), *to determine IEP goals, supports, and services.*
☐	5. In inclusive early childhood education settings, educators and care providers understand that they have a responsibility to *proactively adapt experiences and instruction to accommodate children's differences.*
☐	6. In inclusive early childhood education settings, educators and care providers have had explicit and extensive *professional learning opportunities* to learn about and understand what constitutes *differentiated instruction.*
☐	7. In inclusive early childhood education settings, educators and care providers *presume diversity and gather facts* about all of their learners, along multiple dimensions of diversity (e.g., skills, interests, preferences), *with a focus upon each child's strengths* that sustains his/her engagement in everyday activities and interaction with people and materials.
☐	8. Within inclusive early childhood settings, *content and material differentiation routinely occurs,* with children being provided multiple representations of material to be experienced or learned. Educators and care providers determine and use materials (e.g., building supplies, play structures, toys) and adult interactional and instructional behaviors that are most likely to prompt optimal levels of each child's competence.
☐	9. Within inclusive early childhood settings, *process differentiation routinely occurs* to help children make sense of what they are to do and learn. Educators and care providers use a variety of strengths-based, everyday activities and context-specific instructional

Rating (0 – 4)	Indicator of Student-Centered, Strength-Based Assessment and Differentiated Instruction
	and interactional practices to facilitate children's engagement, learning, and expression of interests and skills.
☐	10. Within inclusive early childhood settings, *product and assessment differentiation routinely occurs,* with children being offered multiple means to express progress and show what they have learned. Educators and care providers monitor and analyze children's learning and progress via formal and informal (e.g., observational, curriculum-based) assessment approaches in order to adjust learning opportunities, as needed.
☐	11. Educators and care providers in inclusive early childhood settings know and routinely *use a systematic process,* such as the Mismatch and Solution-Finding Differentiation Process, to *proactively or reactively* identify and *resolve mismatches* between the instruction that typically has been provided in a classroom and the attributes of children with more diverse learning, communication, behavioral, or other characteristics than team members have been accustomed.

Total Score (out of 44 maximum): ________

Mean Score (Total Score/11): ________

Range of Scores: ______ **(low) to** ______ **(high)**

References

Division for Early Childhood. (2014). *DEC recommended practices in early intervention/early childhood special education 2014.* Retrieved from www.dec-sped.org/recommendedpractices

Falvey, M., Forest, M., Pearpoint, J., & Rosenberg, R., (2002). Building connections. In J. S. Thousand, R. A. Villa, & A. I. Nevin (Eds.), *Creativity & collaborative learning: The practical guide to empowering students, teachers, & families* (2nd ed., pp. 29-54). Baltimore: Paul H. Brookes Publishing Co., Inc.

Gutierrez-Clellen, V. & Peña, E. (2001). Dynamic assessment of diverse children: A tutorial. *Language, Speech, and Hearing Services in Schools, 32,* 212-224.

King, G., Strachan, D., Tucker, M., Duwyn, B., Desserud, S., & Shillington, M. (2009). The application of a transdisciplinary model for early intervention services. *Infants & Young Children, 22*(3).

Moore, S., Hyde-Smith, A., Pratt, C., & McKnight, R. (2011). Pathways to assessment of learning: A family-centered, culturally responsive approach to transdisciplinary assessment in early childhood. *Perspectives on Language Learning and Education, 18*(2), 40– 46. doi:10.1044/lle18.2.40

Myers, C. L., McBride, S. L., & Peterson, C. A. (1996). Transdisciplinary, play-based assessment in early childhood special education: An examination of social validity. *Topics in Early Childhood Special Education, 16*(1), 102.

Thousand, J. S., Villa, R. A., & Nevin, A. I. (2015). *Differentiating instruction: Planning for universal design and teaching for college and career readiness* (2nd ed.). Thousand Oaks, CA: Corwin Press.

Universal Design for Learning (2013). What is it, what it looks like, where to learn more. *The Special EDge, 26*(1), 2-3.

Early Childhood Inclusive Education Best Practice #8:

Multi-Tiered System of Supports (MTSS) for Differentiated, Embedded, Specially Designed, and Targeted Instruction, and Academic, Behavioral, and Social-Emotional Learning

The notion of a Multi-Tiered System of Supports (MTSS) was first introduced in the 2004 reauthorization of the Individuals with Disabilities Education Act (IDEA) as an instructional system for preventing unnecessary special education referral by providing research-based instruction in general education and swift and targeted interventions to accelerate learning of struggling students. Originally termed Response to Intervention (RTI), this system is conceptualized as a three-tiered "pyramid" approach, with Tier 1 being high-quality, evidence-based instruction with universal supports and frequent learner progress monitoring. In early childhood education, Tier 1 supports are intended for all learners and include developmentally appropriate and culturally responsive curriculum and instruction; positive and caring relationships between children and caregivers; and supportive collaborative problem solving among home, school, and community partners (DEC, NAEYC, & National Head Start Association, 2013). Tier 2 supports are intended for learners who need extra support to engage in and benefit from the curriculum. Tier 2 supports include adaptations to and modifications of the curriculum, as well as specially designed and targeted interventions embedded in learning experiences or delivered via small group instruction and guided practice.

Tier 3 supports are for those few children who do not make adequate progress on critical early skills (e.g., language, early literacy, social-emotional) given the supports and interventions provided at Tiers 1 and 2. Tier 3 supports represent intensive (frequent and individualized) interventions designed to enable a child to successfully participate and progress in the curriculum. Interventions may target communication, social-emotional, behavioral, academic, or any other skills deemed critical for a child to meaningfully engage in learning and participate in the learning community. Tier 3 interventions may require small group or one-on-one instruction (Barton, & Smith, 2015). For children exhibiting persistent behaviors that interfere with safe and engaged community participation, Tier 3 supports include a functional behavioral assessment (FBA) and analysis of the behaviors of concern in order to determine the communicative intent of the behavior and the development and implementation of a positive behavior support plan of comprehensive interventions and supports. It should be noted that Tier 3 interventions are not special education or automatic referral for assessment for special education. However, if Tier 3 supports prove ineffective, assessment for special education eligibility may be considered as part of a deeper examination of the child.

Over the past decade, the Multi-Tiered System of Supports or MTSS language has emerged as the umbrella concept and label for a comprehensive system of "high-quality first instruction, supports, and interventions... for all students, regardless of whether they are struggling or have advanced learning needs" (California Services for Technical Assistance and Training, 2015, p. 2). MTSS is an overarching structure for organizing support for the academic and social-emotional-behavioral health and growth of children by automatically differentiating instructional content and materials, products and assessments, and processes of learning based upon the natural learning differences among children. See Chapter 7 of this book and Thousand, Villa, and Nevin (2015) for more on differentiated instruction.

It is noteworthy that the most recent reconceptualization of MTSS expands the umbrella of support and intervention to include social-emotional learning as a third dimension of learning that is co-equal with academics and behavior. Social-emotional learning (SEL) can be defined as the process of acquiring and applying dispositions, knowledge, and skills to understand and manage emotions, empathize, develop relationships, set and accomplish goals, and make responsible decisions (https://casel.org/what-is-sel). For a breakdown of social and emotional learning competencies and SEL research and resources, visit the Collaborative for Academic, Social, and Emotional Learning (CASEL) website (https://casel.org). Also see the California MTSS framework, which aligns academic, behavioral, and social-emotional learning in an integrated system of support for all children (www.ocde.us/MTSS/Pages/CA-MTSS.aspx). Finally, for current research and best practices regarding RTI and MTSS as applied in early childhood education, visit the University of Kansas' Center for Response to Intervention in Early Childhood (www.crtiec.dept.ku.edu).

Early Childhood Inclusive Education Best Practice Checklist Assessment

Best Practice #8:
Multi-Tiered System of Supports (MTSS) for Differentiated, Embedded, Specially Designed, and Targeted Instruction, and Academic, Behavioral, and Social-Emotional Learning

Directions: Based upon your experience, please give each of the 15 indicators a (zero to 4) rating in response to the question, "To what degree does this best practice occur in our early childhood education setting(s)?"

4	3	2	1	0
Always	Most of the time	Some of the time	Rarely	Never

Rating (0 – 4)	Indicator of Multi-Tiered System of Supports (MTSS) for Differentiated, Embedded, Specially Designed, and Targeted Instruction, and Academic, Behavioral, and Social-Emotional Learning
☐	1. Our early childhood education programs (and schools that provide early childhood education services) have a *well-articulated and well-understood Multi-Tiered System of Supports (MTSS)* for academics, behavior, and social-emotional learning.
☐	2. Early childhood education personnel *receive quality training on developmentally appropriate, culturally responsive, evidenced-based curriculum and instruction* for all students.
☐	3. Early childhood education personnel *receive quality training* in *positive behavioral support* approaches.
☐	4. Early childhood education personnel *receive quality training* in *social-emotional learning* and how to facilitate social-emotional learning in natural, routine contexts.

Rating (0 – 4)	Indicator of Multi-Tiered System of Supports (MTSS) for Differentiated, Embedded, Specially Designed, and Targeted Instruction, and Academic, Behavioral, and Social-Emotional Learning
☐	5. Early childhood education personnel provide *high-quality, developmentally appropriate, culturally responsive, evidenced-based instruction* for all students.
☐	6. Early childhood education personnel *deliberately and routinely use positive behavioral supports* to promote a sense of community and safety for all students.
☐	7. Early childhood education personnel *deliberately* focus upon and routinely and effectively *facilitate and embed social-emotional learning* opportunities in experiences throughout the day.
☐	8. Early childhood education personnel *understand and believe* that (most) *behavior is a form of communication,* often about unmet needs.
☐	9. When a child shows recurring or intensified disruptive behavior, our *typical response is a team approach to determine the function of the behavior* in order to develop comprehensive interventions and supports.
☐	10. Our *first step* in developing a positive behavior support plan is to *collect data* about the *child's strengths and other characteristics,* as well as about the *context(s)* in which the troubling behavior occurs (i.e., antecedents and consequences).
☐	11. Home, school, and community partners *routinely engage in collaborative problem-solving* processes when a child needs additional support (i.e., Tier 2 or 3 interventions) beyond the universal supports provided in Tier 1 to engage in and benefit from the curriculum.

Rating (0 – 4)	Indicator of Multi-Tiered System of Supports (MTSS) for Differentiated, Embedded, Specially Designed, and Targeted Instruction, and Academic, Behavioral, and Social-Emotional Learning
☐	12. Early childhood education personnel *adapt and modify curriculum, embed specially designed interventions* in learning experiences, and provide *individual or small group instruction* and guided practice *at increasing levels of intensity* (i.e., Tier 2 and 3 interventions) for students who need extra support to engage in and benefit from the curriculum.
☐	13. Our MTSS system has built-in, *continuous progress monitoring* during Tier 2 and 3 interventions.
☐	14. Our early childhood education personnel *provide Tier 2 and 3 interventions before considering referral* for assessment for special education.
☐	15. We *regularly engage in program evaluation and continuous improvement* of our MTSS system.

Total Score (out of 60 maximum): ______

Mean Score (Total Score/15): ______

Range of Scores: ______ (low) to ______ (high)

References

Barton, E. E., & Smith, B. J. (2015). *The preschool inclusion toolbox: How to build and lead a high-quality program.* Baltimore, MD: Paul H. Brookes Publishing Co., Inc.

California Services for Technical Assistance and Training (2015). A multitiered system of supports with response to interven tion and universal design for learning: Putting it all together (Special insert), *The Special EDge, 28*(2), 1-4.

Division of Early Childhood, National Association for the Education of Young Children, & National Head Start Association. (2013). *Framework for response to intervention in early childhood: Description and implications.* Retrieved from https://cainclusion.org/teachingpyramid/materials/resources/DEC_NAEYC_NHSAJointPaperonRTIinEarlyChildhood_final.pdf

Individuals with Disabilities Education Act (IDEA), 20 U.S.C. § 1400 (2004).

Thousand, J. S., Villa, R. A., & Nevin, A. I. (2015). *Differentiating instruction: Planning for universal design and teaching for college and career readiness (2nd ed.).* Thousand Oaks, CA: Corwin Press.

Early Childhood Inclusive Education Best Practice #9:

Decision-Making Processes for Determining Where, When, and How to Address IEP Goals for Students with Intensive and Pervasive Support Needs

Teams most successful in meaningfully including and addressing IEP goals of children, particularly children with significant and pervasive support needs, use a structured and systematic process such as the nine-step process outlined in Table 9.1. The table identifies each step of the process, and the corresponding early childhood inclusive education best practice and the chapter in which the best practice is described. Three of the steps of the nine-step process (Steps 3 – 5) are the focus of this chapter. In order to gain a full and comprehensive picture of the nine steps working together, we suggest that after reading this chapter, you return, by step, to the chapters that correspond with each step (i.e., for Step 1, return to Chapter 5; for Step 2, return to Chapter 7; etc.) and read about the best practice and its corresponding indicators.

Steps 3, 4, and 5 of the nine-step process are information-sharing and decision-making steps for interfacing a student's IEP goals with the daily activities and schedule of an inclusive early childhood educational environment. These three steps, known as the IEP Goal Activity Decision-Making Process (Thousand & Villa, 1995), guide a child's team through a process of asking and answering a series of four questions and using the IEP at a Glance and IEP Goal Activity Matrix tools to get to know a student and determine where, when, and how to address his/her IEP goals in ways that ensure not only access, but optimal participation and support. A student's IEP team applies this process before considering not placing a child in an inclusive early childhood setting, removing a child from an inclusive early childhood environment, or teaching a child in a non-inclusive learning structure (e.g., one-on-one instruction inside or outside of the classroom, instruction with a group of students, all of whom have IEPs).

Question 1. What are this student's strengths, learning preferences, and priority IEP goals to be emphasized in the inclusive early childhood environment?

As described in Chapter 7, thinking and teaching in a Universal Design for Learning (UDL) way requires educators and care providers to first gather facts about students. For students with IEPs, not only do instructional staff discover information about all students (i.e., learning preferences; social-emotional, academic, language, and cultural characteristics and strengths), they also learn about the priority IEP goals of students eligible for special education. The IEP at a Glance is a communication tool that offers those who work with a student a brief, positive profile of the student, a summary of the student's primary goals, and critical management needs and other important information they need to know (e.g., needed mobility, repositioning, eating supports; positive behavior supports) that allow for safety, health, and optimal participation.

Table 9.2 shows the IEP at a Glance for Danika. Notice that descriptions in her profile are worded in positive terms. For example, rather than characterizing Danika as "stubborn," "willful," or "resistant to direction," her team positively describes her as "assertive about her wants." Also note that, for Danika, an important set of management needs for staff to know and understand are the positive behavior support strategies identified in her Positive Behavior Interventions and Supports (PBIS) Plan. Other critical management needs are for Danika to receive her medication at lunchtime and lifting assistance when using the bathroom toilet.

Question 2. Where and when can a student's objectives be best addressed?

A tool that has been particularly effective in helping teachers interface a student's IEP goals with the daily activities and schedule of an early childhood or any educational environment is the IEP Goal Activity Matrix. Figure 9.1 shows the IEP Goal Activity Matrix completed by Danika's team for the schedule and activities of her early childhood program. Team members first list each of the priority objectives in the left column of the matrix and then, for each activity or part of the day, consider the question, "Could this objective possibly be addressed during this activity?" Note that they do not ask, "Will this objective be addressed during this activity." By asking the first "could possibly" question, team members usually discover not only that IEP goals can be addressed in an inclusive educational environment, but that IEP goals could be addressed in multiple activities across the day. Our experience is that the more practice educators have using a tool such as this matrix, the more creative they become in figuring out when and how IEP goals might be embedded within the routines and activities of an early childhood education program. Once this matrix is completed, then the team is ready to examine the "how" of inclusive schooling by examining and answering Question 3.

Question 3. What adaptations to the content, product, and process of instruction will allow for maximum participation and learning?

Early childhood educators who successfully include students with diverse learning characteristics continually make decisions about what will be adapted, adjusted, reconfigured, streamlined, and clarified in their curriculum, instruction, and assessments. A team always has options for a student to contribute and participate in inclusive early childhood education environments (Giangreco, Cloninger, & Iverson, 2011; Giangreco, Dymond, & Shogren, 2016; Ohtake, 2003). Table 9.3 summarizes four participation options described by Giangreco and colleagues (2011, 2016). The key to (a) determining which participation option to expect of a child in a particular activity, and (b) avoiding underestimating a child's capabilities, is always presuming competence (defined in Chapter 1) and first considering having a student do the same thing as everyone else before proceeding down the list of other participation options.

When considering participation options, the Mismatch and Solution-Finding Differentiation Process described in Chapter 7 can and should be used by educators and early childhood care providers to optimize a child's participation (i.e., with no accommodations needed, multilevel curriculum and instruction, or curriculum overlapping) and avoid the child's exclusion from activities. Further, when considering supports that might be needed for participation, consider peer support before adult support, as research makes very clear that the most effective interventions and supports are those that involve children (Strain & Smith, 2016; Thousand, Villa, & Nevin, 2015).

Question 4. Does an alternative activity need to be designed?

An alternative activity, the last option identified in Table 9.3, can be crafted and employed when answers to the previous questions are not yet sufficient. Because of the research finding that peer involvement is so powerful to the development of young children with IEPs, by design, an alternative activity should, if possible, include a partner or a small group of students without disabilities rather than arranging one-on-one instruction with an adult. Quality alternative activities often are experiential or activity-based and may occur outside of the classroom. At all times, alternative activities should be age and developmentally appropriate and meaningful for the students involved (Villa & Thousand, 1995).

Consider, for example, the following alternative activity crafted for Ellie, a preschooler with an IEP. A trio of preschoolers including Ellie, who is firming up her differentiation of the colors red, yellow, and orange, survey classmates as to which of the three is their favorite color. Ellie is responsible for completing a chart with a column below each of the three colors by placing a tally mark under the color preference of each student queried. Ellie's partners have additional questions they have formulated related to the topic of study—differentiation of colors, numbers, and shapes. After the survey activity, the trio collaborates to count up tally marks; Ellie's partners help her to count and identify which is the most, second, and least preferred color.

There will be times when a student's team deems an inclusive education environment or experience less than optimal for addressing a priority IEP goal. In cases where a student must leave the inclusive setting for a priority purpose, the IEP Goal Activity Matrix again can be used to highlight when (during which activity or activities) removal from the inclusive environment will be least disruptive to the student's social engagement with peers or opportunities to receive embedded instruction on priority IEP goals. For some students, there may be an activity or time of day during which social engagement with peers is minimal or fewer IEP goals can be easily addressed. This activity or time of day may be a priority time for a student to receive one-on-one instruction or needed instruction or services outside of the inclusive classroom. For Danika, the student featured in the Figure 9.1 example, there are few activities in which most of her priority goals cannot be addressed. As with Danika, an IEP team may decide that a student's IEP goals are adequately addressed through incidental learning and direct and embedded instruction in the routines and activities of the inclusive preschool educational program, and that no services need to be delivered outside of inclusive settings. If a team does decide a service needs to be provided outside of an inclusive context, the team will want to consider providing that service at times (e.g., before or after the hours of the child's inclusive early education program) and/or on days that minimally disrupt inclusive program participation.

Deciding to remove a student from an inclusive educational setting and same-aged peers should be a decision of last resort. Applying the IEP Goal Activity Decision-Making Process described in this chapter should minimize the need to deliver services in a non-inclusive environment.

Table 9.1 Nine-Step Process for Implementing and Monitoring IEPs for Children with Significant and Pervasive Support Needs in Inclusive Education Environments and Corresponding Best Practice Chapters

Decision-Making Step	Best Practice Chapter
Step 1. Assemble a team Who should be on a team?	Collaborative teaming (Chapter 5)
Step 2. Gather student data	Student-centered, strength-based assessment and differentiated instruction (Chapter 7)
IEP Goal Activity Decision-Making Process	This chapter—Chapter 9
Step 3. Develop IEP at a Glance student profile	This chapter—Chapter 9
Step 4. Create IEP Goal Activity Matrix	This chapter—Chapter 9
Step 5. Explore participation options	This chapter—Chapter 9
Step 6. Identify and correct mismatches between learner and learning environment	Student-centered, strength-based assessment and differentiated instruction (Chapter 7)
Step 7. Provide professional learning, modeling, coaching, and performance-based feedback	Professional learning and coaching (Chapter 10)
Step 8. Promote natural peer supports	Structuring intentional, sufficient, and supported natural peer interactions (Chapter 6)
Step 9. Monitor the program, services, and IEP goal attainment	Redefining roles and responsibilities (Chapter 3)

Table 9.2 IEP at a Glance for Danika

Student Name: Danika (4 years old) **Positive Student Profile** (Social, academic, language, cultural characteristics; strengths; learning preferences)	**Date:** September 13th **IEP Objectives at a Glance**
• Kinesthetic learner • Enjoys and good at trampoline • Active—moves frequently from one activity to another • Learns well with hands-on materials and activities • Musical—moves and dances to music • Vocalizes loudly when excited • Assertive about her wants • Happy working alone	• Share materials • Take turns in group activities • Transition independently from one activity or environment to another using a picture schedule • Put away materials • Recognize her printed first name • Recognize and differentiate shapes—circle, square, triangle • Use sign language or picture communication system to: - Use functional daily living words - Initiate interactions with peers - Request a partner for play or work - Answer yes/no questions - Answer "what" questions - Indicate need to use the bathroom

Management Needs and Other Important Information

- Use the positive behavior support strategies identified in Danika's Positive Behavior Interventions and Supports plan to calm her when upset
  - Protests by vocalizing loudly and refuses when expected to clean up or put away materials
  - Takes materials she wants from other students
  - Sometimes takes her clothes off and runs around the classroom
- Have nurse administer medication at mealtime
- Provide assistance (lifting) to use bathroom toilet

Table 9.3 Four Participation Options

No Accommodations Needed *No accommodations needed* is a participation option when a student can do the same as everyone else or basically the same with minor modifications or supports (classmate support, preferential seating, positioning, extended time, reduced amount) typically available in a classroom. **Multilevel Curriculum and Instruction** *Multilevel curriculum and instruction* is a second option where all students are involved in a lesson in the same curriculum area, but are pursuing varying objectives at multiple levels based upon their unique needs. For example, in math, students can work on number quantity skills at varying levels. Some students may compare greater and fewer objects, some may order written numerals of single-digits and others with two to three-digit numbers, others may label quantities by counting objects, and yet others may be learning the verbal names for number quantities 1 and 2 as well as colors by imitating a peer, cross-aged tutor, or adult's reading of the number labeling and counting of objects on each page of Dr. Seuss' *One Fish, Two Fish, Red Fish, Blue Fish.* **Curriculum Overlapping** *Curriculum overlapping* is a third option that involves students working on the same lesson, but pursuing objectives from different curricular areas. For example, Alena, a preschooler with significant and pervasive support needs, is working in a cooperative group with two other students, using the lap tray attached to her wheelchair as the team's workspace. Most students are engaged in a preschool weather science experiment, Rain Cloud in a Jar (described at https://funlearningforkids.com/rain-cloud-jar-science-experiment/). They are expected to follow the steps of the experiment and predict, observe, and record findings in words and/or pictures. Alena is expected to identify the color of

(continued on next page . . .)

Table 9.3 (continued)

the water in two of the four small jars placed on her lap tray. It was determined that this was also an excellent opportunity to address Alena's other IEP objectives from the curriculum areas of communication and socialization.

One communication objective (i.e., object discrimination) was simple for Alena's lab partners to facilitate throughout the experiment. Another motor goal—maintain and increase range of motion—was achieved by students using hand-under-hand assistance so Alena could pass group members the pipettes needed to gather drops of colored water from four small jars and place them into the larger jar that contained shaving cream. Caution is advised with respect to moving to curriculum overlapping as a participation option without first exploring how Universal Design for Learning principles might be used to proactively design lessons that build in multiple forms of representation, engagement, and expression, which enable all students to engage with the curriculum in different ways.

Alternative Activities

Alternate activities may be needed in a student's schedule to allow for management needs (e.g., catheterization in the nurse's office requiring privacy) or when an education activity cannot be adapted or is deemed by the student's IEP team as not best met in the inclusive environment (e.g., district-wide screenings; one-on-one discrete-trial training requiring a quiet, distraction-free environment with a specially trained Applied Behavior Analysis specialist). Once again, caution is advised when deciding to remove a student from an inclusive educational setting. Private time for elimination is one activity for which students need privacy. Other things can typically happen during natural breaks during the day. Some students carry bags with a G-tube so they can have nutrition according to their schedule but do not have to miss the content covered throughout the school day.

Figure 9.1 IEP Goal Activity Matrix for Danika and Her Half-Day Early Childhood Program

Name: Danika **Date: September 13**

IEP Goals	Activities									
	Arrival	Free Choice Time	Morning Meeting (Schedule/ Literacy Focus)	Station Rotations (Literacy Focus)	Morning Mealtime	Recess	Large Group Activity (Arts Focus)	Station Rotations (Math/ Science Focus)	Large Group Closing Activity	Departure
Share materials		X		X		X	X	X		
Take turns in groups		X	X	X	X	X	X	X	X	X
Transition between activities/ environments	X	X	X	X	X	X	X	X	X	X
Put away materials		X		X	X	X	X	X		X
Recognize written first name	X		X	X	X			X		X
Recognize shapes	X	X	X	X	X	X	X	X		X
Use daily living words*	X	X	X	X	X	X	X	X	X	X
Initiate peer interactions*	X	X		X	X	X		X		X
Request play/work partner*		X		X	X	X	X	X		X
Answer yes/no questions*	X	X	X	X	X	X	X	X	X	X
Answer "what" questions*	X	X	X	X	X	X	X	X	X	X
Indicate need to use bathroom*					X	X			X	X
Management Needs and Other Important Information										
Use PBS strategies to calm when in distress	X	X	X	X	X	X	X	X	X	X
Medication at mealtime					X					
Lifting assistance in bathroom	X				X	X				X

* Using sign language or picture communication system

Early Childhood Inclusive Education Best Practice Checklist Assessment

Best Practice #9:
Decision-Making Processes for Determining Where, When, and How to Address IEP Goals for Students with Intensive and Pervasive Support Needs

Directions: Based upon your experience, please give each of the 9 indicators a (zero to 4) rating in response to the question, "To what degree does this best practice occur in our early childhood education setting(s)?"

4	3	2	1	0
Always	Most of the time	Some of the time	Rarely	Never

Rating (0 – 4)	Indicator of Processes for Determining Where, When, and How to Address IEP Goals for Students with Intensive and Pervasive Support Needs
☐	1. Inclusive early childhood personnel *view effective differentiated instruction as the foundation* on which to build and provide inclusive educational services.
☐	2. A child's *special education classification* or eligibility category (e.g., intellectual disability, multiple disabilities, deaf-blindness, autism) *does NOT determine or limit the expectations* that educational, care provider, related services, and other personnel have for that student.
☐	3. IEP teams of young children with disabilities, particularly students with intensive and pervasive support needs, *use a process similar to the Nine-Step Process* shown in Table 10.1 to *implement and monitor inclusive* Individual Education Programs (IEPs) for children in inclusive early childhood educational environments.

Rating (0 – 4)	Indicator of Processes for Determining Where, When, and How to Address IEP Goals for Students with Intensive and Pervasive Support Needs
☐	4. IEP teams for young children with disabilities, particularly students with intensive and pervasive support needs, *use a tool such as the IEP at a Glance to communicate* in a brief and concise format a positive profile of each student's characteristics, as well as priority goals, safety and health management needs, and other important information team members need to know to facilitate each child's successful inclusive educational experience.
☐	5. IEP teams for young children with disabilities, particularly students with intensive and pervasive support needs, *use a decision-making process such as the IEP Goal Activity Decision-Making Process* to determine where, when, and how to address priority IEP goals in inclusive early childhood education environments in ways that ensure not only access, but optimal participation and support in learning.
☐	6. IEP teams *presume competence* of all students and consider participation options identified in Table 10.2., *first considering having a student do the same thing as everyone else* before considering the other options.
☐	7. For every young child with an IEP, IEP team members *consider* the *multilevel curriculum and instruction and curriculum overlapping* participation options described in Table 10.2 *prior* to considering and creating an *alternative activity* or removing a child from an inclusive early childhood setting.
☐	8. Students' *IEP teams apply a decision-making process* such as the IEP Goal Activity Decision-Making Process *BEFORE:* (a) *deciding not to place a child in an inclusive early childhood education setting,* (b) *removing a child from an early childhood inclusive education setting,* or (c) *teaching* a child in a *non-inclusive learning structure*

Rating (0 – 4)	Indicator of Processes for Determining Where, When, and How to Address IEP Goals for Students with Intensive and Pervasive Support Needs
	(e.g., one-on-one instruction inside or outside of the classroom; instruction with a group of students all of whom have IEPs).
☐	9. Educators and care providers of young children with disabilities *use a process* such as the Mismatch and Solution-Finding Differentiation Process (described in Chapter 7) *to adapt content, product, and process demands* of activities so children with and without IEPs can successfully engage in the first three participation options described in Table 10.2.

Total Score (out of 36 maximum): ________

Mean Score (Total Score/9): ________

Range of Scores: ______ **(low) to** ______ **(high)**

References

Giangreco, M. F., Cloninger, C. H., & Iverson, V. S. (2011). *Choosing outcomes and accommodations for children (COACH): A guide to educational planning for students with disabilities* (3rd ed.). Baltimore, MD: Paul H. Brookes Publishing Co., Inc.

Giangreco, M. F., Dymond, S. K., Shogren, K. A. (2016). Educating students with severe disabilities: Foundational concepts and practices. In F. Brown, J. McDonnell, & M. E. Snell (Eds.) *Instruction of students with severe disabilities* (8th ed, pp. 1-26). Boston, MA: Pearson.

Ohtake, Y. (2003). Increasing class membership of students with severe disabilities through contribution to classmates' learning. *Research and Practice for Persons with Severe Disabilities, 28,* 228 – 231.

Strain, P. S., & Smith, L. (2016, February 18). Preschool inclusion: What's the evidence, what gets in the way, and what do high-quality programs look like? [Webinar] In 2016 *National Inclusion Webinar Series of the Early Childhood Technical Assistance Center.* Retrieved from http://ectacenter.org/~calls/2016/nationalinclusion.asp

Thousand, J. S., Villa, R. A., & Nevin, A. I. (2015). *Differentiating instruction: Planning for universal design and teaching for college and career readiness* (2nd ed.). Thousand Oaks, CA: Corwin Press.

Villa, R. A., & Thousand, J. S. (1995). *Creating an inclusive school.* Alexandria, VA: Association for Supervision and Curriculum Development.

10

Early Childhood Inclusive Education Best Practice #10:

Professional Learning and Coaching

It is well recognized that a barrier to effectively serving young children with disabilities in community early child care and educational settings is the lack of professional development for and expertise within the early childhood workforce (Barton & Smith, 2015; U.S. Department of Health and Human Services & U.S. Department of Education, 2015). Considering the need to construct a coordinated early childhood professional development system, the Institute of Medicine and National Research Council (2015) recommends that, at a minimum, everyone working with young children share common knowledge in: (a) child development and learning, (b) the importance of consistent and nurturing relationships, and (c) biological and environmental factors that influence development. Additionally, they recommend everyone acquire competence to: (d) engage children in high-quality interactions, (e) facilitate social-emotional development and minimize challenging behavior, (f) recognize when a child may need assessment and/or additional services, and (g) use various differentiated methods to promote learning.

Building upon this set of foundational knowledge and skills, the U.S. Department of Health and Human Services and U.S. Department of Education (2015) further argue for professional learning that leads to positive attitudes and beliefs about inclusion and disability, the use of culturally and linguistically responsive practices, and the principles and practices of Universal Design for Learning (see Chapter 7). They state that training in these areas is essential for all personnel[1], from administrators to paraeducators.

Professional development on a theory or practice does not ensure implementation of that theory or practice. Famously, Joyce and Showers (2002) have found that "0% of teachers will use a practice in their classrooms following training in the theory and discussion of the practices. . . . However, 95% will use the practice in their classroom if they receive ongoing coaching" (Barton & Smith, p. 99). More specifically, Joyce and Showers have found that knowledge and skill regarding a new instructional practice increase when demonstrations are also provided in the training. Knowledge and skill increase further when opportunities for guided practice and feedback are provided during the training. However, actual classroom use is likely to occur only if ongoing coaching is provided.

Confirming the value of coaching, in their synthesis of implementation research, Fixsen, Naoom, Blase, Friedman, and Wallace (2005) found participants in training to be most likely to incorporate a new practice into their daily instructional routine if, following training, they receive coaching and performance-based feedback. Surveying early childhood educators, Dunst and Rabb (2010) found that preschool teachers reported greater learning from on-site coaching than from workshop training alone.

Given the importance of modeling, guided practice, and coaching in turning theory into practice for educators, the rating scale for this Professional Learning and Coaching best practice is constructed in a different format from the other chapters.

---

[1]The U.S. Department of Health and Human Services and U.S. Department of Education (2015) identify as among all staff, "LEA administrators, early childhood program directors, school principals, family child care network leaders, teachers and providers, early interventionists, early childhood special educators, related services providers, other specialized providers, and aides" (p. 16).

The scale not only assesses whether professional learning on a topic has or has not been provided, but also the degree to which a professional learning experience that includes lecture and discussion is supplemented with: (a) the presentation of live or video modeling and demonstrations, (b) opportunities for participant guided practice, and (c) opportunities for onsite observation, coaching, and performance-based feedback. Please score an indicator with "0" if no training opportunities have been provided with regard to the indicators. Score "1" if a professional learning experience has been provided and it included only lecture and discussion. Score "2" if the experience also included live or video modeling and demonstrations. Score "3" if the experience additionally included guided practice in using the focus practice(s). Score "4" if, following training, observations with coaching and performance-based feedback were provided. The scale, as modified for this Professional Learning and Coaching best practice, is shown below.

4	3	2	1	0
On-Site Coaching	**Guided Practice During Training**	**Demonstration & Modeling**	**Lecture & Discussion**	**No Training Opportunity**

The 14 topical areas included and assessed on the following pages are not exhaustive. State departments of education, local education agencies (LEAs), early childhood programs, supporting agencies, and your own team may have deemed important additional professional learning experiences that forward inclusive early childhood education that supplement or complement those already identified in this Chapter 10 checklist. Therefore, space has been provided to allow for the addition and rating of up to six additional professional learning topics.

Early Childhood Inclusive Education Best Practice Checklist Assessment

Best Practice #10:
Professional Learning and Coaching

Directions: Based upon your experience, please give each of the 14 indicators a rating (zero to 4) that best represents the quality of your professional learning experience(s) regarding the professional learning topic represented by the indicator.

4	3	2	1	0
On-Site Coaching	**Guided Practice During Training**	**Demonstration & Modeling**	**Lecture & Discussion**	**No Training Opportunity**

Rating (0 – 4) **Topical Indicator of Professional Learning and Coaching**

Using the 5-point Likert scale (0 -4) above, please rate the degree to which you have received high-quality professional development in . . .

☐ 1. inclusive early childhood education (e.g., what it is, the *research supporting inclusion*—see Best Practice #1 in Chapter 1).

☐ 2. *child development and learning*, biological and environmental factors that influence development, early childhood pedagogy.

☐ 3. the importance of and *strategies for forming* strong consistent and nurturing *relationships* with children and their families.

☐ 4. *culturally and linguistically responsive practices,* such as learning about and using a family's cultural, linguistic, and other dimensions of diversity in interacting with and planning for their child's educational program.

☐ 5. how to *engage children in high-quality interactions* and facilitate positive relationships among all students

Rating (0 – 4)	Topical Indicator of Professional Learning and Coaching
	and facilitate natural peer-to-peer supports and peer-mediated intervention.
☐	6. *social-emotional development,* the facilitation of social-emotional learning, and use of positive behavior supports to minimize challenging behavior.
☐	7. how to recognize when a child may need assessment and/or additional support services via *ongoing developmental monitoring,* strength-based assessment, and universal developmental and behavioral screenings.
☐	8. the *use of various methods* (e.g., prompting, modeling, reinforcement, visual supports, teaching, and reinforcing routines) for promoting learning in all activities (e.g., free and outdoor play, learning groups, snack, circle time).
☐	9. collaborative planning, creative problem solving, and home-school-community *collaboration.*
☐	10. *co-teaching* among early childhood educators and care providers, early childhood special educators and other interventionists, related service personnel (e.g., speech pathologist), health specialists, and others to facilitate student access to the content being taught.
☐	11. the use of *evidence-based practices* such as embedding IEP goal instruction into natural routines, cooperative and partner learning structures, and the use of augmentative and assistive technology.
☐	12. *differentiated instruction,* accommodations and modifications, principles and practices of Universal Design for Learning (UDL).
☐	13. how to *train and supervise paraeducators* to provide learning support to students with disabilities, other students who struggle in learning, and all students in an early childhood setting.

Rating (0 – 4)	Topical Indicator of Professional Learning and Coaching
☐	14. the *legal rights of families and responsibilities of educators* and other service providers with regard to IEP eligibility determination, goal setting, service delivery, progress monitoring, and transition planning.

Total Score (out of 56 maximum): ________

Mean Score (Total Score/14): ________

Range of Scores: ______ **(low) to** ______ **(high)**

Additional Topical Indicators

Directions: Are there additional professional learning topics that your state, LEA, program, agency, or team have deemed important to enhance the inclusive education of young children with disabilities? Identify the topic and give it a rating (zero to 4) that best represents the quality of the professional learning experience.

4	3	2	1	0
On-Site Coaching	Guided Practice During Training	Demonstration & Modeling	Lecture & Discussion	No Training Opportunity

Rating (0 – 4) **Additional Topical Indicator of Professional Learning and Coaching**

Using the 5-point Likert scale (0 -4) scale above, please rate the degree to which you have received high-quality professional development in . . .

Rating	Indicator
☐	15.
☐	16.
☐	17.
☐	18.

☐ 19.

☐ 20.

Total Score (out of ____ maximum): ________

Mean Score (Total Score/____): ________

Range of Scores: ______ (low) to ______ (high)

References

Barton, E. E., & Smith, B. J. (2015). *The preschool inclusion toolbox: How to build and lead a high-quality program.* Baltimore, MD: Paul H. Brookes Publishing Co., Inc.

Dunst, C. J., & Raab, M. (2010). Practitioners' self-evaluation of contrasting types of professional development. *Journal of Early Intervention, 32,* 239-254.

Fixsen, D. L., Naoom, S. F., Blase, K. A., Friedman, R. M., & Wallace, F. (2005). *Implementation research: A synthesis of the literature* (FMHI Publication #231). Tampa, FL: University of South Florida, Louis de la Parte Florida Mental Health Institute, National Implementation Research Network. Retrieved from https://nirn.fpg.unc.edu/sites/nirn.fpg.unc.../files/.../NIRN-MonographFull-01-2005.pdf

IOM (Institute of Medicine) & NRC (National Research Council). (2015). *Transforming the workforce for children birth through age 8: A unifying foundation.* Washington, D.C.: The National Academies Press.

Joyce, B. R., & Showers, B. (2002). *Student achievement through staff development* (3rd ed.). Alexandria, VA: Association for Supervision and Curriculum Development.

U.S. Department of Health and Human Services & U.S. Department of Education. (2015, September 14). *Policy statement on inclusion of children with disabilities in early childhood programs.* Washington, DC: Authors.

11

Early Childhood Inclusive Education Best Practice #11:

Administrative Practices Supportive of Inclusive Early Childhood Education

Administrative leadership and support is central to achieving the beneficial outcomes of early childhood inclusive education. What does administrative leadership look like and sound like? It looks and sounds like local education agencies (LEAs) (i.e., school districts), administrators, early childhood directors, principals, and family child care leaders articulating and building consensus for an inclusive vision of all young children being welcomed, valued, empowered, and supported in learning social-emotional, language and communication, and academic skills in shared environments and experiences. It sounds like administrators clarifying for program personnel how inclusive early childhood education relates to and supports other best practices such as co-teaching, differentiated instruction, positive behavior supports, a focus upon social-emotional learning, facilitating natural peer support, and embedding IEP goal instruction within natural routines (Villa & Thousand, 2017). It looks like arranging time so that early childhood instructional personnel (e.g., early childhood care providers; early childhood special educators; specialized supports and related service personnel, such as speech and language pathologists) and other community partners can collaborate in planning and teaching.

Administrative leadership also looks and sounds like systematic professional development that includes coaching and mentorship so that early childhood instructional personnel and community partners learn and practice skills in collaborative planning and effective and differentiated instruction for young children with and without IEPs. Administrative leadership looks and sounds like crafting and delivering meaningful incentives to encourage early childhood instructional personnel and community partners to learn and use new instructional and behavior support approaches. Administrative leadership looks like the reorganization of human resources to encourage shared responsibility for all students among all early childhood educators and providers by modifying the allocation of funds that serve young children with disabilities, and establishing staffing structures that blend the expertise of skilled early childhood educators and providers with the expertise of specialized personnel (e.g., early childhood special educators, related service personnel). Finally, administrative leadership looks and sounds like moving people through a systematic and transparent action planning and implementation process regarding vision, skills, incentives, and resources so that inclusive early childhood educational practices occur with integrity.

Early Childhood Inclusive Education Best Practice Checklist Assessment

Best Practice #11:
Administrative Practices Supportive of Inclusive Early Childhood Education

Directions: Based upon your experience, please give each of the 12 indicators a (zero to 4) rating in response to the question, "To what degree does this best practice occur in pur early childhood education setting(s)?"

4	3	2	1	0
Always	**Most of the time**	**Some of the time**	**Rarely**	**Never**

Rating (0 – 4)	Indicator of Administrative Practices Supportive of Inclusive Early Childhood Education
☐	1. *LEAs establish formal agreements* with early childhood programs and service providers in the community to ensure *alignment and delivery of comprehensive inclusive services* for young children with and without IEPs.
☐	2. In order to effect continuous improvement in instruction and address the learning of all young children, early childhood programs serving young children with IEPs conduct *ongoing developmental monitoring, universal development and behavioral screenings, and follow-up,* as needed.
☐	3. LEA and community early childhood program partner administrators *regularly and publicly convey a commitment to and rationale for inclusive education* and the practices that support it (e.g., collaborative planning, co-teaching, collaboration with families, differentiating instruction). Administrators make explicit connections between inclusive early childhood education and other improvement initiatives and the overarching inclusive vision for all young children.

Rating (0 - 4)	Indicator of Administrative Practices Supportive of Inclusive Early Childhood Education
☐	4. *School and community members are kept appraised* (e.g. via website, newsletters, reports, presentations to the school board) of the *accomplishments* of inclusive early childhood education endeavors and partnerships.
☐	5. *Professional learning* to create common conceptual language and frameworks, skills, and dispositions (e.g., workshops, courses, mentoring and coaching, Professional Learning Communities, book studies, job shadowing, pairing of new collaborating and teaching teams with veteran collaborators) among personnel of school- and community-based early childhood programs and care providers *has occurred and is ongoing.*
☐	6. LEAs and other programs with dedicated professional development funds, such as Head Start, make *professional learning regarding inclusive early childhood education available* not only to their own personnel, but to the personnel of other local early childhood, child care, and family care providers.
☐	7. LEA and community early childhood program partner administrators systematically *determine the collaboration needs of personnel* (e.g., With whom do various personnel need to collaborate? For what purposes? How often?).
☐	8. LEA and community early childhood program partner administrators actively coordinate their actions to ensure school and community early childhood personnel who need to collaborate to plan for the instruction and continuous performance monitoring of young children with and without disabilities are regularly *provided with adequate time* (e.g., release time built into the work schedule and routine) *to collaboratively plan and problem solve.*

Rating (0 - 4)	Indicator of Administrative Practices Supportive of Inclusive Early Childhood Education
☐	9. In addition to planning time, *administrators provide incentives* (e.g., recognition for efforts and accomplishments of collaborators, provision of coaching, provision of release time to observe one another in action, sending teams to conferences, teams asked to make presentations about their accomplishments) *for collaborative planning and problem solving.*
☐	10. *Roles* of all school- and community-based early childhood program personnel and care providers have been *redefined so that everyone is expected to collaborate* to educate the diverse group of learners with and without IEPs receiving early childhood educational services.
☐	11. Least Restrictive Environment (LRE) mandates and *inclusive practices* (e.g., collaboration in planning and teaching, differentiated instruction) are included and *addressed in the evaluations of personnel* providing instructional and other support services to young children with IEPs.
☐	12. LEA and community early childhood program partner administrators facilitate a systematic and transparent *action planning* and implementation process of goal setting and progress monitoring *regarding vision, skills, incentives, and resources* for creating, sustaining, and improving inclusive early childhood education.

Total Score (out of 48 maximum): ________

Mean Score (Total Score/12): ________

Range of Scores: ______ **(low) to** ______ **(high)**

References

Villa, R. A., & Thousand, J. S. (2017). *Leading an inclusive school: Access and success for ALL students.* Alexandria, VA: Association for Supervision and Curriculum Development.

12

Early Childhood Inclusive Education Best Practice #12:

Transition Planning from Part C (Birth to Three) to Part B (Three to Five) Services, and from Part B (Three to Five) to School-Aged Services

By the time young children with disabilities enter elementary school, they and their families likely will have made many transitions across and among services, service providers, and settings. Transitions occur across the day, such as moving from home to child care to preschool, and across time, such as moving at age three from early intervention (i.e., IDEA Part C) to public school (i.e., IDEA Part B) programs and services. All of these transitions present opportunities and challenges and involve changes for children and families, which may be experienced differently from one family to the next based upon the child and family's cultural and linguistic background, previous experiences with transitions, and age and level of development of the child. Without careful planning, transitions can result in uncertainty and concern on the part of families, and fewer opportunities for a child's current and future participation in age-appropriate general education and integrated community activities. When early childhood education programs, schools, and community organizations are careful and deliberate in their collaboration during times of transition, they create continuity for families and across systems (DEC/NAEYC, 2009; U.S. Department of Health and Human Services & U.S. Department of Education, 2015).

Transition planning involves a host of stakeholders, including a child's parents or guardians, educators, and care providers representing all of the sending and receiving programs and settings in which the child has spent, is spending, or will spend time. Transition planning provides families and educators the opportunity to set goals for the next learning environments and experiences and make connections with the teachers and service providers in the next setting(s). To best facilitate transitions, anticipate problems, provide interventions, and allow for federal IDEA assessment and eligibility determination timelines (e.g., holding the IEP meeting within 60 days of a signed assessment plan) to be met, the planning process should occur well in advance of the actual transition. For example, IDEA requires that, when transitioning a child from Part C, birth to three services, to Part B, special education services, transition planning can begin as early as nine months but no later than three months prior to a child's third birthday.

Family-driven, student-centered planning is a transition planning approach that specifically focuses upon future outcomes and the quality of life and dreams of those who care most about a child and who are responsible for a child's education and care. Making Action Plans (Villa, Thousand, & Nevin, 2010) and Pathways: A Child and Family Journey© (Moore, Hyde-Smith, Pratt, & McKnight, 2011) are examples of person-centered planning processes that engage a wide circle of people (including the child, when possible) in thinking about a child's history, attributes and gifts, and their dreams and fears for the child's future, in order to create a plan that moves toward dreams and avoids fears/concerns. Family-driven, student-centered transition planning plays an important role in preparing for the future lives and goals of children with disabilities and, therefore, should start early and be an expected part of every transition throughout a child's schooling.

Early Childhood Inclusive Education Best Practice Checklist Assessment

Best Practice #12:
Transition Planning from Part C (Birth to Three) to Part B (Three to Five) Services, and from Part B (Three to Five) to School-Aged Services

Directions: Based upon your experience, please give each of the 12 indicators a (zero to 4) rating in response to the question, "To what degree does this best practice occur in our early childhood education setting(s)?"

4	3	2	1	0
Always	**Most of the time**	**Some of the time**	**Rarely**	**Never**

Rating (0 – 4) **Indicator of Transition Planning**

☐ 1. The local education agency (LEA) and early childhood education programs, schools, and community service partners have established *transition policies and procedures* detailing how they will collaborate and provide continuity for children and families as they move through transitions.

☐ 2. The LEA and providers responsible for educational services for young children with disabilities use *well-defined planning processes to facilitate successful transition* of these children and families to the various new settings, services, and personnel responsible for providing educational and other supports.

☐ 3. The *transition planning process* for a young child with disabilities is *collaborative,* with a child's educators, family members, involved related services and community agency and partner personnel, the child (when possible and appropriate), and anyone important in the student's life (e.g., extended family members, family friends) actively sought out, invited, and involved in the process.

Rating (0 – 4)	Indicator of Transition Planning
☐	4. The *transition planning process* is a *family-driven, person-centered* process that focuses a child's team on the child's *history, strengths, preferences, dreams, needs,* and *present levels of performance,* as well as the family and team members' *dreams and concerns* for the child's future, in order to identify goals and provide services and supports that lead to the dreams and avoid the fears/concerns. (See Chapter 7 for family-driven, person-centered processes such as MAPs and Pathways.)
☐	5. A major emphasis of transition planning is the continuation and *expansion over time of inclusive educational opportunities.*
☐	6. Throughout the transition planning process, current educators, service providers, and family members *share with new service providers the supports and services* that have *proven to be effective* with a child (e.g., assessment results, behavior intervention plans, assistive technology supports) so their use is transferred to the new program.
☐	7. Leadership of the LEA, early childhood education programs, schools, and community service partners have discussed and come to mutual understandings and agreements on how to best *align curricula, teaching strategies, environments, and learning expectations* between the educational *experiences* and settings that *precede* and *follow* a child's transition.
☐	8. The LEA, schools, and other local early intervention service providers review *transition processes to ensure that natural environments and inclusive settings* (i.e., those settings considered for children without disabilities) *are meaningfully considered* (i.e., families are not given an either/or option—you may choose Head Start or special education) for each infant,

Rating (0 – 4)	Indicator of Transition Planning
	toddler, and preschooler with a disability transitioning into subsequent educational programs.
☐	9. As part of the transition process, each *family is provided* with and guided through *an accessible* (e.g., in lay language, with clear and simple checklists, in family's primary language) *handbook*, such as the *When I'm 3, where will I be? – A Family's Transition Workbook* (www.isbe.net/Documents/transition_workbook.pdf), *that identifies key steps of the transition process*, responsibilities of sending and receiving programs, and family support resources.
☐	10. As part of the transition planning process and prior to placement decisions, *families* are provided with opportunities to *visit all possible future placement options* and encouraged to bring along a support person (e.g., another parent of a child with disabilities, a family member or friend, a current service provider) to discuss their visits.
☐	11. As part of the transition process, *early childhood educational programs* have established and *employ positive and enjoyable trasition traditions* (e.g., creating a memory book, going on an "adventure" to the new classroom).
☐	12. In order to improve transition processes, *leadership* of LEAs, early education programs, schools, and community service partners *assess* (e.g., via survey, interview) *family*/primary caregivers' perceptions of and *satisfaction with transitions* after transitions occur.

Total Score (out of 48 maximum): ________

Mean Score (Total Score/12): ________

Range of Scores: ______ **(low) to** ______ **(high)**

References

Division of Early Childhood/National Association for the Education of Young Children (DEC/NAEYC). (2009). *Early childhood inclusion: A joint position statement of the Division for Early Childhood (DEC) and the National Association for the Education of Young Children (NAEYC).* Chapel Hill, NC: The University of North Carolina, FPG Child Development Institute.

Illinois Birth-5 Transition Guidance Committee. (n.d.). *When I am 3, where will I be? – A family's transition workbook.* Springfield, IL: Illinois State Board of Education. Retrieved at www.isbe.net/Documents/transition_workbook.pdf

Individuals with Disabilities Education Act (IDEA), 20 U.S.C. § 1400 (2004).

Moore, S., Hyde-Smith, A., Pratt, C., & McKnight, R. (2011). Pathways to assessment of learning: A family-centered, culturally responsive approach to transdisciplinary assessment in early childhood. *Perspectives on Language Learning and Education, 18*(2), 40– 46. doi:10.1044/lle18.2.40

U.S. Department of Health and Human Services & U.S. Depart ment of Education. (2015, September 14). *Policy statement on inclusion of children with disabilities in early childhood programs.* Washington, DC: Authors.

Villa, R. A., Thousand, J. S., & Nevin, A. I. (2010). *Collaborating with students in instruction and decision making: The untapped resource.* Thousand Oaks, CA: Corwin Press.

13 Early Childhood Inclusive Education Best Practice #13:

Continuous Planning for Sustainability

Continuous effective planning for installing, expanding, and sustaining an inclusive education vision and set of best practices requires attention to at least five variables: vision, skills, incentives, resources, and action planning (Lindsey, Thousand, Jew, & Piowlski, 2018; Villa & Thousand 2005, 2017). These five variables need to be planned for and visited periodically for goal and activity adjustment, and assessment of the integrity and progress of a school's implementation and sustainability plan. Table 13.1 describes the actions that need to be taken to forward and sustain an inclusive (or any) education philosophy and practice. Figure 13.1 provides an Early Childhood Inclusive Education Action Plan template for teams to use to set goals for and monitor progress in creating, sustaining, and improving inclusive early childhood education options.

Complacency—thinking that and acting as if you have "arrived" and do not need to tend to a change effort—can be the most harmful barrier to sustaining any change. It can stifle the maintenance of an inclusive vision and quality inclusive practices. Creating inclusive early childhood environments is a long-term commitment that requires eternal vigilance. Change agents, no matter what the initiative, must: articulate the vision for new personnel and partners every year they come on board; provide continuous, high quality professional learning and coaching opportunities; maintain incentives (e.g., celebrating innovators, creating time for collaboration); provide human and other resource allocations; and engage in ongoing planning and assessment of the quality of early childhood inclusive educational experiences for everyone.

Table 13.1 Five Requisite Variables and Associated Actions for Continuous Improvement and Sustainability

Variable	Associated Actions
Vision	Articulate and build consensus for a vision of inclusive early childhood education and home-school-community collaboration.
Skills	Develop educator, community agency personnel, administrator, paraeducator, and parent knowledge, skills, and confidence for implementing quality early childhood inclusive education best practices through professional learning experiences and coaching.
Incentives	Create and implement a menu of meaningful incentives (e.g., extra collaborative planning time, professional learning opportunities, opportunities to share successes with others) for personnel to take risks to try something new to implement early childhood inclusive education.
Resources	Expand and sustain human, technological, fiscal, and organizational resources to implement early childhood inclusive education.
Action Planning	Engage in ongoing planning and data collection to assess the quality of early childhood inclusive education throughout the process of change.

Figure 13.1 Early Childhood Inclusive Education Action Plan

Community and School District:______________________					
Our Community's Early Childhood Inclusive Education Vision:					
Goals by Change Variable • What goals do we need to address and achieve for each variable? • To what extent does the goal align with the vision statement? • Is the goal written using SMART criteria (defined at the bottom of this figure)?	**Actions** • List actions chrono-logically • Include preparation (e.g., funding) and implemen-tation actions	**Success Measure(s)** "We will know we are successful if/when..." • What is measured? • Who will measure? • When to measure?	**Person(s) Responsible**	**Date by Which to be Achieved**	**Actual Outcomes:**
VISION **Instilling and Installing a Vision of Early Childhood Inclusive Education** What goals do we need to set to attain this outcome?					
Goal One:	**Actions to Achieve Goal One:**	**Success Measure(s):**	**Person(s) Responsible:**	**Date:**	**Outcomes:**
Goal Two:	**Actions to Achieve Goal Two:**	**Success Measure(s):**	**Person(s) Responsible:**	**Date:**	**Outcomes:**
SKILLS **Building Skills and Capacity for Serving Students With and Without IEPs in Early Childhood Inclusive Education Settings** What goals do we need to set to attain this outcome?					
Goal One:	**Actions to Achieve Goal One:**	**Success Measure(s):**	**Person(s) Responsible:**	**Date:**	**Outcomes:**
Goal Two:	**Actions to Achieve Goal Two:**	**Success Measure(s):**	**Person(s) Responsible:**	**Date:**	**Outcomes:**

(continued on next page . . .)

Figure 13.1 (continued)

INCENTIVES

Providing Incentives to Engage People in Creating, Sustaining, and Improving Early Childhood Inclusive Education

What goals do we need to set to attain this outcome?

Goal One:	Actions to Achieve Goal One:	Success Measure(s):	Person(s) Responsible:	Date:	Outcomes:
Goal Two:	**Actions to Achieve Goal Two:**	**Success Measure(s):**	**Person(s) Responsible:**	**Date:**	**Outcomes:**

RESOURCES

Orchestrating Human, Technological, Fiscal, and Organizational Resources for Creating, Sustaining, and Improving Early Childhood Inclusive Education

What goals do we need to set to attain this outcome?

Goal One:	Actions to Achieve Goal One:	Success Measure(s):	Person(s) Responsible:	Date:	Outcomes:
Goal Two:	**Actions to Achieve Goal Two:**	**Success Measure(s):**	**Person(s) Responsible:**	**Date:**	**Outcomes:**

SMART Goals:

Specific = Who, what, when, where, which, why?

Measurable = Concrete criteria for measuring success: How much, how many, how will we know?

Attainable = What do we need to be successful? What knowledge, skills, attitudes, and/or resources do we need to develop to attain the goal?

Realistic = Is our goal set high enough and are we willing to work hard enough to reach it?

Timely & Tangible = What is our sense of urgency? Do we have a timeline with short- and long-term actions to achieve the goal? Can we picture the outcome? Do we know when we have reached the goal?

Early Childhood Inclusive Education Best Practice Checklist Assessment

Best Practice #13:
Self-Assessment:
Continuous Planning for Sustainability

Directions: Based upon your experience, please give each of the 9 indicators a (zero to 4) rating in response to the question, "To what degree does this best practice occur in our early childhood education setting(s)?"

4	3	2	1	0
Always	**Most of the time**	**Some of the time**	**Rarely**	**Never**

Rating (0 – 4)	Indicator of Continuous Planning for Sustainability
☐	1. *At least annually,* following an assessment of the implementation of quality early childhood inclusive education practices (using an assessment such as this Early Childhood Inclusive Education Checklist), our school district and community partners *develop, monitor, and update goals and activities* on a *measurable early childhood inclusive education improvement plan.*
☐	2. The district and community's *early childhood inclusive education improvement plan is based upon an analysis of assessment data* regarding: a) the extent to which best practices (e.g., the practices and indicators included in this Early Childhood Inclusive Education Checklist) are implemented; and b) student performance, as well as other sources of feedback from early childhood education and school personnel, families, and community partners.
☐	3. In order to clarify roles of participating parties and ensure alignment and delivery of comprehensive services to young children with and without

Rating (0 – 4)	Indicator of Continuous Planning for Sustainability
	disabilities in inclusive learning environments, the district and community's *early childhood inclusive education improvement plan is widely disseminated* in accessible formats and explained to early childhood and school personnel, families, and community members.
☐	4. The district and community's early childhood inclusive education improvement plan includes strategies to: a) *build consensus for the vision* of educating students of mixed ability in inclusive early childhood education settings and programs; b) *build professional capacity* and skills of early childhood education personnel to effectively collaborate in planning and teaching, use positive behavior supports and evidence-based and differentiated instruction methodologies and assessment practices; and c) maintain and *enhance collaboration* among school, families, and community partners.
☐	5. The district and community's early childhood inclusive education improvement plan *has clear and measurable activities and timelines* for improving best practices.
☐	6. The district and community's early childhood inclusive education improvement plan *includes meaningful incentives for personnel to take risks to try new things* to implement inclusive practices (e.g., professional learning opportunities, planning time, sharing successes at conferences), and adequate resources (human, technological, fiscal, and organizational) to sustain and expand inclusive early childhood education services.
☐	7. The district and community's early childhood inclusive education improvement plan *allows for at least annual adjustments in caseloads* and collaborative

Rating (0 – 4)	Indicator of Continuous Planning for Sustainability
	teaming *and co-teaching configurations* based upon anticipated student support needs.
☐	8. A *team* comprised of district, community partner, and parent representatives *meets regularly to monitor progress* on implementing the early childhood inclusive education improvement plan *and make necessary adjustments* to activities and timelines to achieve planned outcomes.
☐	9. A factor considered and assessed during the process of *hiring new instructional and administrative personnel* is the candidate's *knowledge of* and *commitment to* early childhood *inclusive education* best practices.

Total Score (out of 36 maximum): ________

Mean Score (Total Score/9): ________

Range of Scores: ______ **(low) to** ______ **(high)**

References

Lindsey, D. B., Thousand, J. S., Jew, C. J., & Piowlski, L. R. (2018). *Culturally proficient inclusive schools: All means ALL!* Thousand Oaks, CA: Corwin Press.

Villa, R. & Thousand, J. (2005). *Creating an inclusive school* (2nd ed.). Alexandria, VA: Association for Supervision and Curriculum Development.

Villa, R. & Thousand, J. (2017). *Leading the inclusive school: Access and success for ALL students.* Alexandria, VA: Association for Supervision and Curriculum Development.